on track ...

The Smiths & Morrissey

every album, every song

Tommy Gunnarsson

SONICBOND

sonicbondpublishing.com

Sonicbond Publishing Limited
www.sonicbondpublishing.co.uk
Email: info@sonicbondpublishing.co.uk

First Published in the United Kingdom 2021
First Published in the United States 2021

British Library Cataloguing in Publication Data:
A Catalogue record for this book is available from the British Library

ISBN 978-1-78952-140-5

Typeset in ITC Garamond & ITC Avant Garde
Printed and bound in England

Graphic design and typesetting: Full Moon Media

on track ...

The Smiths & Morrissey

every album, every song

Tommy Gunnarsson

SONICBOND

sonicbondpublishing.com

This book is for Anna and Tage.

Acknowledgements

First of all, thanks to Stephen for giving me this opportunity and for all the great advice along the way, and to Lisa Torem for being a great sounding board. Other people really worth mentioning are Annika, John, Hanne, and of course my brother and my mum. Thanks for being so supportive!

on track ...

The Smiths & Morrisey

Contents

Foreword

The Smiths. They were far from the first guitar-based pop group, and they were not the last either. I think we all can agree on that. But it's impossible to ignore their importance and influence on pop music in general – indie-pop in particular – since their demise more than 30 years ago. Every once in a while a 'new Morrissey' or a 'new Marr' emerges on the worldwide pop scene. Though sometimes a far-fetched reference, this is all too often a rather fitting description. So, why are we still obsessing over a band that only managed to release four studio albums in as many years, and then split up? Why is it that the world of pop just can't seem to forget the names Morrissey, Johnny Marr, Andy Rourke and Mike Joyce?

I think there are many possible explanations, but since we don't want to end up with a book as thick as a brick, I won't delve too deep into that for now. I think it's fair to say that two of the main reasons for their enormous legacy are the songwriting of Morrissey and Marr, and also the former's undeniable charisma. The singer and the guitarist are now hailed as one of the greatest songwriting duos in music history, up there with Lennon and McCartney, Jagger and Richards, and Goffin and King – even though they were never quite the hit machines that the aforementioned pairs were.

Compared to other indie bands at the time, The Smiths actually had some chart success as well, which isn't that surprising listening to their singles, although the albums were also very successful in the UK charts. They are accessible, to say the least, which wasn't something you could say about most of their label mates at Rough Trade (don't get me wrong – I love a lot of the Rough Trade acts – but they weren't really aiming for the pop charts), and as Morrissey maintained from day one that fame was his priority in life, you have to say that he succeeded in that.

But The Smiths didn't just influence the youth of the 80s musically. Even in the band's early days, Morrissey championed his heroes – from authors to actors to musicians. On promo shots, he was often seen clutching a copy of an Oscar Wilde book, and his lyrics were more often than not crammed with quotes and 'thefts' from movies and plays – especially if you listen to their first singles and albums, with the record covers always featuring one of those heroes. All in all, Morrissey did what he could to make sure that the memory of his heroes would live on into the 21st century.

I mentioned how The Smiths influenced the indiepop scene of the following decades, but even more, they were a huge influence – if not the major one together with the Beatles– on the britpop scene that exploded in the mid-90s. Bands like Gene were crowned 'the new Smiths', and their singer Martin Rossiter even got the nickname 'Roz', which of course was a play on Morrissey's nickname 'Moz'.

I think it's fair to say that pop music from the 80s and onwards wouldn't have been the same if Marr never had knocked on Morrissey's door on Kings Road and asked if he wanted to write some songs with him...

Part One: The Smiths

Early Singles

Hand in Glove (single, 1983)

Personnel:
Morrissey: vocals
Johnny Marr: electric guitar, harmonica
Andy Rourke: bass guitar
Mike Joyce: drums

'Hand in Glove' (Morrissey/Marr)
So, here it is – the debut single! Morrissey himself once said in an interview with the magazine *Star Hits*, that the line 'Yes, we may be hidden by rags / But we've something they'll never have' was his favourite among his own lyrics, and also telling them of his desire to use the theme of complete loneliness. Marr, on the other hand, later said that he thought that the song was about him and Morrissey. The latter's idol Sandie Shaw also recorded a cover version in 1984, backed by The Smiths (minus Morrissey). The single version has a fade-in and fade-out, and Rourke's bass is a bit louder in the mix here. The version later included on the album was remixed by John Porter from the original tapes, recorded in 10cc's Strawberry Studios in early 1983, and has a cold start.

'Handsome Devil' (Morrissey/Marr)
This B-side was recorded live at the Hacienda in Manchester on February 4th, 1983. The lyrics made this one of the songs accused of having pedophilic tendencies (most likely because of the lines 'A boy in the bush is worth two in the hand / I think I can help you get through your exams / Oh, you handsome devil'), but Morrissey insisted that the 'essence of the song' was in the final two lines – the now-classic: 'There's more to life than books, you know / But not much more.' I'm not quite sure what he meant by that, but it's a great song and a good example of the more energetic early Smiths sound. A recording of the song from the band's first Peel Session in May 1983 was later included on the *Hatful of Hollow* compilation.

This Charming Man (single, 1983)

Personnel:
Morrissey: vocals
Johnny Marr: guitars, harmonica
Andy Rourke: bass guitar
Mike Joyce: drums

'This Charming Man' (Morrissey/Marr)
Originally written for a session recorded for John Peel's show on BBC radio one in September 1983, it became The Smiths' second single when it replaced

'Reel Around the Fountain', which was initially slated for that slot. It was probably the first real 'pop hit' the band had, being their first single to enter the charts (peaking at 25), and when it was re-released to coincide with the release of the 'Best...' compilations in 1992, it became their highest-charting single ever in the UK (at eight). Lyrically, it tells the story of a man who gets a flat tire on his bike and then gets a lift by a 'charming man' in a 'charming car', a man who eventually asks the biking guy out that night. However, the biker declines the offer, as he hasn't 'got a stitch to wear'. It was not included on the original release of the debut album in the UK but was later added on the US release, and since then, it has been added on all reissues, both US and non-US.

'Jeane' (Morrissey/Marr)

This is actually the only recording made with original album producer Troy Tate that was officially released, and it's surprisingly non-jangly for an early Smiths song. Indeed, Marr has revealed in later interviews that he did try to get away from the band's trademark jangle when he wrote this song. It was originally played at a slower pace until Morrissey insisted that they should speed it up a little. The 'Jeane' in the song has been rumoured to be Morrissey's old friend Linder Sterling, but it could be any one of his adolescent friends, really. The song was later covered by Sandie Shaw (as a B-side to her 'Hand in Glove' single in 1984) and modern-day protest singer Billy Bragg.

'Accept Yourself' (Morrissey/Marr)

This song was planned to be included on the debut album at the time of the recordings with Troy Tate that were later scrapped, but was later placed on this B-side instead when it was re-recorded with John Porter. The lyrics are pretty straightforward, with Morrissey telling the listeners to be themselves, no matter what. Musically, Marr has admitted that he was heavily inspired by Tamla Motown in general and The Four Tops in particular, which is quite audible in his guitar playing on this song.

'Wonderful Woman' (Morrissey/Marr)

Yet another song that is reportedly about Linder Sterling, this one was originally called 'What Do You See in Him?', with completely different lyrics, but later transformed into this lovely song. Morrissey later admitted that the song was about a woman who was quite the opposite of 'wonderful', but despite her horrible ways, he would still forgive her. The song was recorded with Troy Tate, but this version is the re-recording done with John Porter.

The Smiths (1984)

Personnel:
Morrissey: vocals
Johnny Marr: electric guitar, acoustic guitar, harmonica
Andy Rourke: bass guitar
Mike Joyce: drums, tambourine
Paul Carrack: piano, organ (on 'Reel Around the Fountain', 'You've Got Everything Now' and 'I Don't Owe You Anything')
Annalisa Jablonska: voice ('Pretty Girls Make Graves' and 'Suffer Little Children')
Caryn Gough: sleeve layout
Morrissey: sleeve concept
Joe Dallesandro: cover star
Recorded at Pluto (Manchester), Strawberry (Stockport), Eden (London), Matrix (London)
John Porter: producer (except 'Hand in Glove'), remixer ('Hand in Glove')
The Smiths: producers ('Hand in Glove')
Playing time: 45:36
Label: Rough Trade
Release date: February 20th 1984
Highest chart position: UK: 2

After releasing their acclaimed debut single 'Hand in Glove' in 1983, the pressure was surely on for the four members of The Smiths. Their label Rough Trade had extremely high hopes for their newest find, and pop fans all over the UK thought that their upcoming debut album would be something really spectacular. And they had every reason to believe so. The songs were there, the band was good, and gaining a reputation as a live act. But it didn't turn out quite as everyone expected.

After signing with Rough Trade, the band released the debut single and were soon preparing to enter the studio to record their first full-length record. The label boss, Geoff Travis, suggested that they might use Troy Tate (former guitarist with The Teardrop Explodes, whose frontman Julian Cope would later have a few minor hits of his own) as their producer, and since the band hardly had any experience in the studio, they thought that it sounded great. Sadly, the recordings they made with Tate (fourteen songs in all) were deemed to be too bad to release – they just didn't seem to capture the band's energetic live sound in a good way. After a remix was considered, the tapes were thrown away – though they have been released on unofficial bootlegs every now and then. Morrissey and his bandmates instead asked John Porter (who they met while recording a session for the BBC) to save the day. While his recordings was more acceptable, the recordings are far from great. Listening to the album now, it sounds really dense, quite far from the energetic live recordings available from the same period. Even Morrissey thought that it wasn't good enough to put out, but since the recordings had been more expensive than planned, he had no choice. Being Morrissey, however, he went on to describe the album as a 'landmark in the history of pop' in the promotional interviews for the record.

Keeping in the tradition of having cult stars on their covers, Morrissey chose a photo of actor Joe Dallesandro, taken from Andy Warhol's movie *Flesh* (1968), to decorate the front sleeve. The picture of a topless man also helped spark the flame of his associations with gay culture that would haunt Morrissey for more or less the rest of his career. But the main controversies surrounding this album would instead involve children.

'Reel Around the Fountain' (Morrissey/Marr)

The album kicks off with one of those controversial songs, with lyrics that were reportedly pedophilic (the B-side of 'Hand in Glove', 'Handsome Devil', was also accused of the same tendencies). Sure, the line 'It's time the tale was told / Of how you took a child / And you made him old' may suggest something sinister, but the accusation seems a bit far-fetched. Morrissey strongly denied the accusation, and it blew over. While talking about the lyrics, it's worth mentioning the line 'You can pin and mount me like a butterfly', which is supposedly a reference to John Fowles novel *The Collector* from 1963 (whose movie adaptation would provide the cover shot to the next Smiths single, 'What Difference Does It Make?'), and also 'I dreamt about you last night and I fell out of bed twice', which is basically taken straight out of Shelagh Delaney's excellent play (and later movie), *A Taste of Honey* (1958). Musically, the song starts off with Joyce's steady drumbeat and then evolves into one of the slower songs on the album. The song also features one of the rare guest appearances on a Smiths record, as Paul Carrack (at that time playing with Nick Lowe, but also a member of Ace, Squeeze and Mike and The Mechanics) plays the piano and organ. Morrissey's former girlfriend, Annalisa Jablonska, also adds some backing vocals. The song was originally planned to be The Smiths' second single, but when the label heard the new song 'This Charming Man', which the band recorded for a John Peel session, they changed their mind.

'You've Got Everything Now' (Morrissey/Marr)

This, a fairly straightforward pop song, features some really classic Morrissey lyrics, 'I've never had a job / Because I never wanted one', and 'I don't want a lover / I just want to be seen in the back of your car.' In interviews, he often talked about how he could never imagine working for a living (that is, having a 'regular' job), and this song is surely a comment on this, as well as on how he saw the world around him turning more and more materialistic, and that riches don't make people happy ('I've seen you smile / But I never really heard you laugh').

'Miserable Lie' (Morrissey/Marr)

This early live favourite starts out slowly, but then suddenly changes tempo and finishes at a much more furious pace. Lyrically, songs like these were part of the reason why the journalists at the time (and the fans) started wondering whether Morrissey's lyrics were autobiographical or not. Some of them obviously weren't, but when writing about losing the love of your life or about the longing for love, it all seemed a lot closer to home. Lines like 'I know I need hardly say / How much I love your casual way / Oh, but please put your tongue away' and 'I need advice / Nobody ever looks at me twice' (the latter sung in a somewhat stretched falsetto – no wonder the band always used to close their live sets with this one) sure sound like something that might have happened in young Steven's life.

'Pretty Girls Make Graves' (Morrissey/Marr)
Taking its title from Jack Kerouac's *The Dharma Bums*, the lyrics reverse a more traditional (but nevertheless sad) situation as a girl pressures her boyfriend into having sex with her, though he ends up losing her anyway: 'Then on the sand / Another man, he takes her hand /... / I lost my faith in womanhood.' Curiously, Morrissey then ends up quoting himself in the song's coda, when he wails, 'Hand in glove / The sun shines out of our behinds'. The version of the song recorded with Troy Tate later surfaced in 1987 when it was released as a B-side to the single 'I Started Something I Couldn't Finish' (from the album *Strangeways, Here We Come),* with cello provided by Audrey Riley.

'The Hand That Rocks the Cradle' (Morrissey/Marr)
Originally meant to be the album's title track (it was planned to be called 'The Hand That Rocks the Cradle' during the Troy Tate sessions), this is another one of the alleged 'pedophilic' lyrics. And sure, if you listen closely, lines like 'There's sadness in your beautiful eyes / Oh, your untouched, unsoiled, wondrous eyes' and 'Climb upon me knee, sonny boy / Although you're only three, sonny boy / You're – you're mine / And your mother she just never knew' (the latter inspired by Al Jolson's 'Sonny Boy') could be interpreted as being about a man who's having deeply inappropriate thoughts about a young child. But Morrissey also writes from the eyes of a child, with a lot of disturbing images that could be taken from a horror movie – a piano playing in an empty room, bloody cleavers, wavering shadows. The song was one of the very first Morrissey and Marr wrote together and was featured on the first demo they made with temporary drummer Simon Wolstencroft in the summer of 1982 (together with 'Suffer Little Children') before Rourke and Joyce joined the band. It was also one of three songs played during their live debut on October 4th that same year.

'This Charming Man' (Morrissey/Marr)
This, one of the band's most famous songs, was not included on the original UK release of the album, but since it was thrown in on the US release and on all the subsequent reissues, I decided to include it here as well. See 'This Charming Man' single for details.

'Still Ill' (Morrissey/Marr)

This was another one of those early live favourites, and the band kept playing it more or less to the bitter end. You could easily think that the lyrics are referring to the hypochondriac tendencies of Morrissey, and that might as well be true. But it has also been interpreted as being about him realizing that the dreams he once had were now dead and gone, and there's also a healthy dose of the typical Morrissey pessimism: 'And if you must go to work tomorrow / Well, if I were you I really wouldn't bother / For there are brighter sides to life / And I should know because I've seen them / But not very often.' Even Encyclopedia Britannica concludes that 'songs such as 'Still Ill', 'sealed [Morrissey's] role as spokesman for disaffected youth'. The song is still played frequently live by both Morrissey and Marr and was also included in the first Peel session.

'Hand in Glove' (Morrissey/Marr)

(see 'Hand in Glove' single)

'What Difference Does It Make?' (Morrissey/Marr)

This would become The Smiths' third single and became their biggest hit to date (#12 in the UK singles charts), but it was quite obvious that the band weren't too happy with it. The usual Morrissey hype interviews were absent, and the band soon dropped the song from their live setlists. It's also commonly accepted that the version recorded for the Peel session is far superior to the one on the album and single, as the Peel recording managed to capture the band's live energy in a much better way. The cover for the single originally featured an image from the movie adaptation of *The Collector* with actor Terence Stamp, but since he objected to the use of the image on the sleeve, the label printed a new one, where Morrissey replicates Stamp's pose. Stamp later changed his mind, and his image returned again.

'I Don't Owe You Anything' (Morrissey/Marr)

Even though Mike Joyce once claimed that this song was 'one of the most powerful songs that Morrissey had ever done', I think you would have to search for a long time to find a Smiths fan that holds this as her or his favourite. With that being said, it's a good song, and it was also recorded by Sandie Shaw as the B-side to her 'Hand in Glove' single.

'Suffer Little Children' (Morrissey/Marr)

The album's closing track was one of the oldest songs in The Smiths canon (recorded with original bass player Dale as 'Over the Moors') and also one of the most controversial. The lyrics are about the horrible Moors Murders, that were carried out by Myra Hindley and Ian Brady in and about Manchester in 1963-1965. Five children were kidnapped and murdered, and most of the bodies were buried on the Saddleworth Moor. Being the same age as the victims and also being a kid in Manchester at the same time as them, Morrissey was very affected by it all, which shows in the lyrics. Some of the families of the victims didn't like that Morrissey had written a song about their murdered family members, so the album was banned from sale in many of the UK record shops. When Morrissey insisted that his lyrics were meant as a tribute to the children, and also met with the families, they withdrew their complaints, and the singer even became friends with one of the mothers. The song is one of the band's most powerful, both lyrically and musically, although the band played it live just once.

Contemporary Singles

Heaven Knows I'm Miserable Now (single, 1984)

Personnel:
Morrissey: vocals
Johnny Marr: guitars
Andy Rourke: bass guitar
Mike Joyce: drums, tambourine

'Heaven Knows I'm Miserable Now' (Morrissey/Marr)

With a title inspired by Sandie Shaw's 'Heaven Knows I'm Missing Him Now' (1969), this was the band's fourth single when it was released on May 21st 1984 (peaking at #10 in the UK). There's a common 'misunderstanding' among non-fans that Morrissey is a miserable fellow, and this title is probably one of the reasons for that, even though the lyrics are far from his darkest; rather the opposite, actually. The lyrics once again concern a relationship waiting to happen (or is it?), with the narrator admitting shyness shy around his romantic interest ('What she asked of me at the end of the day / Caligula would have blushed / 'You've been in the house too long', she said / And I naturally fled'). Marr's light and airy melody is absolutely gorgeous, and it's no wonder that this is one of The Smiths' best-loved songs. There was some controversy surrounding the single, as the B-side was 'Suffer Little Children', the song about the Moors Murders taken from the debut album, and it was also fueled by the fact that the cover star, Viv Nicholson (who rose to UK fame in 1961 when her husband won a lot of money on the football pools, and then they spent it all in a short period of time), resembled Myra Hindley, on the photo on the single sleeve.

'Suffer Little Children' (Morrissey/Marr)

(see *The Smiths* album)

'Girl Afraid' (Morrissey/Marr)

This is another one of those 'hidden gems' that finally got the attention it deserved when it was included on the *Hatful of Hollow* compilation. If not, 'Girl Afraid' might just have been a forgotten B-side on the 12' version of this single. The song was written by Marr on the same day that he wrote its A-side, and he has said that he considers them to be a pair, which you can almost hear when listening to them back-to-back. Lyrically, Morrissey has explained that he wanted to write a song about the fact that just because you're in a relationship with someone, it doesn't mean you know everything about each other.

William, It Was Really Nothing (single, 1984)

Personnel:
Morrissey: vocals
Johnny Marr: guitars
Andy Rourke: bass guitar
Mike Joyce: drums

'William, It Was Really Nothing' (Morrissey/Marr)

According to Morrissey, the song is about a man speaking to another man, and telling him that marriage is 'really nothing', that it's a waste of time. He thought that all pop songs that concerned marriage were written from the female point of view and that it was about time that the male perspective got some attention. It's widely believed that Morrissey borrowed a lot of the lyrics, at least the theme of them, from one of his favourite novels, *Billy Liar* by Keith Waterhouse, and the opening lines are classic Morrissey: 'The rain falls hard on a humdrum town / This town has dragged you down.' There were also rumours that the song was about Billy Mackenzie (singer in The Associates, a brilliant Scottish post-punk/new wave band), who was friends with Morrissey for a short while. The Associates later recorded a song called 'Stephen, You're Really Something', which was meant as a reply to The Smiths song (though they misspelt Morrissey's name). The single peaked at #17 in the UK singles chart, and both the 7' and 12' had classic Smiths songs as their B-sides ('Please, Please, Please Let Me Get What I Want' and 'How Soon Is Now?', which later made it to the charts again as an A-side). The original sleeve art was taken from an ad for ADS Speakers, but due to legal reasons, it was later replaced with a photo of actress Billie Whitelaw.

'Please, Please, Please Let Me Get What I Want' (Morrissey/Marr)

The shortest song in the entire Smiths catalogue (1:50) is also one of the most beloved, with its lullaby-like melody, and Morrissey yet again singing about the longing for love that has eluded him. The decision to put the song on this B-side was later called 'sinful' by Morrissey, but it's probably one of the most played Smiths songs, at least judging from its inclusions in movies and TV series, and also by the number cover versions that have been recorded of it. The first band to release a cover of it was the British trio The Dream Academy (who had a big hit with their debut single, 'Life in a Northern Town' in 1985), who made the song a minute longer and released it as a single in 1986, when it was featured in the teen comedy *Ferris Bueller's Day Off*.

'How Soon Is Now?' (Morrissey/Marr)

Even though it's not really representative of their sound, I think this song is a serious contender for 'best known Smiths song', with its repetitive, danceable beat and trembling guitars (an effect that was created using some real studio wizardry from both Marr and John Porter). Label boss Geoff Travis thought the song wasn't good enough for being an A-side, while producer Porter thought that it could be a hit, and the song was soon picked up by the UK radio stations and was a while later one of the most requested tracks on several BBC shows. In November 1984, 'How Soon Is Now?' came out as an A-side single in the US, and a few months later, in January 1985, it was finally released as such in the UK as well, eventually peaking at #24 (its relatively lowly position is probably explained by the fact that every Smiths fan already had the song on the previous releases). The song was famously recorded by Marr, Rourke and Joyce while stoned and with the studio flooded in red light to create a suitable atmosphere for the music. And I think I have to mention these immortal Morrissey lines too: 'There's a club if you'd like to go / You could meet somebody who really loves you / So you go, and you stand on your own / And you leave and your own / And you go home, and you cry / And you want to die.'

How Soon Is Now? (single, 1985)

Personnel:
Morrissey: vocals
Johnny Marr: guitars, piano
Andy Rourke: bass guitar, cello
Mike Joyce: drums

'How Soon Is Now?' (Morrissey/Marr)
(see 'William, It Was Really Nothing' single)

'Well I Wonder' (Morrissey/Marr)
(see *Meat Is Murder* album)

'Oscillate Wildly' (Morrissey/Marr)

The songwriting credit for this song is for both Moz and Marr, even though the former just contributed the title for this instrumental (one of the three non-vocal songs the band released, the other two being 'Money Changes Everything' and 'The Draize Train'). According to both the singer and the guitarist, Morrissey encouraged Marr to write and record a song without him writing any words to it, and I would say that it worked out quite well this time. The melody is heavily based on the piano, played by Marr, also writing the song on the upright piano that came with his new house in Bowdon. Rourke can also be heard playing the cello, a rarity on recordings by The Smiths.

Meat Is Murder (1985)

Personnel:
Morrissey: vocals
Johnny Marr: guitars, piano, slide guitar, sound effects ('Well I Wonder')
Andy Rourke: bass guitar
Mike Joyce: drums, tambourine
Caryn Gough: sleeve layout
Paul Slattery: group photo
Toshi Yajima: Morrissey photo
Recorded at Amazon (Liverpool), and Ridge Farm (Surrey)
Produced by The Smiths
Stephen Street: engineer, sound effects ('Rusholme Ruffians', 'I Want the One I Can't Have', 'Meat Is Murder')
Playing time: 39:46
Label: Rough Trade (UK), Sire (US)
Release date: February 11th 1985
Highest chart position: UK: 1

Almost to the day a year after the release of the debut album, The Smiths' second album came out, once again on Rough Trade and Sire in the US, and between the two albums they even managed to squeeze in the very popular compilation *Hatful of Hollow*, which compiled the singles, radio sessions and some live tracks. It's covered in more detail later.

This time, the band decided to produce the record themselves, but they were assisted by engineer Stephen Street (who would later produce most Blur albums, and also records for The Cranberries and Kaiser Chiefs, among others), who they met while recording the single 'Heaven Knows I'm Miserable Now', which came out as the band's fourth single in May 1984.

In the year between *The Smiths* and *Meat Is Murder*, Morrissey had become quite a public figure in the UK, with the newspapers and magazines revelling in his extremely quotable replies in interviews. Following the both critically acclaimed and commercially successful singles released between the albums ('Heaven Knows I'm Miserable Now', 'William, It Was Really Nothing' and 'How Soon Is Now?'), the expectations were high this time around as well, and if the first album was a disappointment when it came to the production, *Meat Is Murder* did a lot better in that respect.

Maintaining the tradition of having controversies surrounding their albums, this time it was the album's title (and title track) that became the focal point, maybe for more obvious reasons than the controversies on the debut. Morrissey was an outspoken supporter of animal rights, and *Meat Is Murder* was his way to help the cause and maybe get a few of his fans to turn to a plant-based lifestyle.

This second album also marked a change to the band's sound, as they began incorporating different influences in their songs, most notably rockabilly, but also some funk on 'Barbarism Begins at Home', which was a sign of a maturing band that had finally found their niche in the UK music scene. Despite this, Marr later told *Guitar Magazine* that he thought that *Meat Is Murder* was his least favourite among The Smiths albums, as he thought that some of the songs were played too fast.

'The Headmaster Ritual' (Morrissey/Marr)
Johnny Marr once told author Johnny Rogan that this song was the one that took him the longest time to finish among all the songs he wrote for The Smiths, and its origins can be traced back to the sessions with Troy Tate for the first album. And there's no denying that it's a great song, both musically and lyrically, from Marr's opening riff to Andy Rourke's magnificent bass line and on to Morrissey's emotional lyrics about tyrannical teachers. For anyone who has read the latter's autobiography (with the self-explanatory title *Autobiography*), it will come as no surprise that these lyrics are considered to be more or less about his school days at St Mary's Secondary School in Stretford, Manchester.

'Rusholme Ruffians' (Morrissey/Marr)
This is actually the first sign of the rockabilly influence that would later appear on future Smiths albums and, perhaps more strikingly, in Morrissey's solo career in the 90s. The song is undoubtedly inspired by the track 'His Latest Flame', written by Doc Pomus and Mort Shuman in 1961 (it was first recorded by Del Shannon, but Elvis Presley had a bigger hit with it later that year), and Marr never made this a secret, as they even played a medley of the two songs in concert. And if the music was clearly influenced by another song, then so were the lyrics, which owed quite a lot to the song 'Fourteen Again' by British comedian and musician Victoria Wood (her lines 'For a promise of a snog the last of the fair / French kissing as kiosks shut / Behind the generators with your coconut / The coloured lights reflected in the Brylcream on his hair' is not far from what Morrissey writes in his lyrics, only his words are a bit darker). Oh, and Rusholme is an area in Manchester, a few miles south of the city centre.

'I Want the One I Can't Have' (Morrissey/Marr)
This is yet another one of those Smiths songs that it's hard to imagine that anyone would hold as their all-time favourite, but that doesn't mean that it's a weak song, which might also say something about the overall quality of their material. According to Mike Joyce, the song was more or less written in the studio as a jam, which must be considered a rare thing for the band. In the lyrics, Morrissey tells someone that he's waiting for 'the day that your mentality / Catches up with your biology', and returns to the line 'It's written all over my face'.

'That Joke Isn't Funny Anymore' (Morrissey/Marr)
Johnny Marr has in interviews been saying that this is one of his favourite Smiths songs, and while I don't really agree with him about its quality, it's still a

smashing song. Morrissey has stated over the years that the song was an answer to all the journalists who asked the same questions over and over and also tried their very best to prove that he was a 'fake', that he wasn't the 'real deal'. Marr's haunting arrangement combines both acoustic and electric guitars in a beautiful way, and Rourke's intricate bass lines make the song even better. The coda, with Morrissey wailing over Marr's sliding and trembling guitars, is just amazing. This was the second single released from the album, in July 1985, and peaked on #49 on the UK charts (but fared better in Ireland, where it peaked at #20).

'How Soon Is Now?' (Morrissey/Marr)
As was the case with 'This Charming Man' on the first album, 'How Soon Is Now?' wasn't included on the original UK release of 'Meat Is Murder', but it was featured on the original US release and also appeared on subsequent reissues on CD and LP in the 90s when Warner acquired The Smiths back catalogue. More on the song on the 'William, It Was Really Nothing' single.

'Nowhere Fast' (Morrissey/Marr)
So, we're back in rockabilly land for this nice little boogie rocker, where Morrissey for the first time badmouthed the British royal family in a song (he had been talking negatively about them in interviews for quite some time, though), a 'tradition' he would keep up on the next album. Apart from mocking the Queen by dropping his trousers in front of her, Morrissey also gives us a regular dose of depressive thoughts: 'And when I'm lying in my bed / I think about life / And I think about death / And neither one particularly appeals to me.'

'Well I Wonder' (Morrissey/Marr)
This is actually a favourite of mine – with its soft, acoustic backing and Morrissey's nostalgic and touching lyrics. He's writing about someone he can't get out of his head ('Please keep me in mind'). The sound effects of rain add to the sadness, too. The song was also the B-side to 'How Soon Is Now?' when it was released as a single in January 1985, which made it the first song to be revealed from *Meat Is Murder*.

'Barbarism Begins at Home' (Morrissey/Marr)
Next stop – Funky Town! While Morrissey sings about child abuse and domestic violence, the rest of the band turns into a funk unit, probably influenced by The Freak Party, Marr's and Rourke's former band, which was knee-deep in the funk. If you ever meet someone who wonders what Rourke ever did for The Smiths, play them this song. His bass line moves the whole song forward, and when Marr stops playing guitar after more than six minutes, the bass and drums keep going for a while longer (there are several clips online of the band playing this live, where Marr takes off his guitar and dances with

Morrissey for the last minute). 'Barbarism' was first played live as early as 1983, and was more or less a constant during the forthcoming tours, where the band extended the song to as much as twice its recorded length, in true funk fashion. The song was also the subject of one of pop history's weirdest duets, as Pete Burns (singer with pop band Dead or Alive, best know for 'You Spin Me Round') joined them on stage at the Royal Albert Hall in London on the 1985 tour. The song was also released as a single in Germany and Italy in April 1985, and then in the UK in 1988 as a CD single.

'Meat Is Murder' (Morrissey/Marr)

Here it is, then – the controversial title track. No prizes for guessing the subject of the song, and this is indeed one of the most straightforward lyrics that Morrissey has ever written. Unsurprisingly, Morrissey had been a vegetarian since his youth, and this was his chance to tell his fans that they should follow his lead when it came to their diets. The song begins with a long intro, where Stephen Street turned a BBC *Sound Effects* album featuring recordings of cows (handed to him by Morrissey) and some additional recordings of machines into a harrowing and creepy slaughterhouse (he slowed it all down for extra effect). After a while, a backwards piano enters the soundscape, and soon the rest of the band joins in to create this atmospheric and powerful hymn to vegetarianism and animal rights. Andy Rourke once told Mojo magazine that he found the song hypnotic and that it still gave him goosebumps, and I can only agree with him. It's hard not to be affected when Morrissey sings lines like 'This beautiful creature must die / A death for no reason / And death for no reason is murder' and 'Kitchen aromas aren't very homely / It's not 'comforting', 'cheery' or 'kind' / It's sizzling blood and the unholy stench of MURDER', before leaving us with the rhetorical question 'Who hears when animals cry?' A lot of youngsters in the UK turned vegetarian after hearing this song, and it's not hard to understand why. On his later solo tours, Morrissey has played the song live while showing footage from slaughterhouses on the backdrop, which has once again caused some controversy.

Contemporary Singles

Shakespeare's Sister (single, 1985)

Personnel:
Morrissey: vocals
Johnny Marr: guitars, piano
Andy Rourke: bass guitar
Mike Joyce: drums

'Shakespeare's Sister' (Morrissey/Marr)

This was the band's seventh single, released on March 18th 1985 (peaking at #26 in the UK). It's another one of those rockabilly influenced tunes the band recorded, and the lyrics are once again influenced by Elizabeth Smart (see

'London'), whilst also taking a few bits from Billy Fury's 'Don't Jump' from 1962, which is about a man standing at the edge of the cliffs, looking down at the rocks below. Morrissey once said that the song was 'really about shrugging off the skins of one's parents and getting out and living and doing what one wants to do'. Apart from the suicidal tendencies of the lyrics, Morrissey also finds the time to sneak in a little attack on men with acoustic guitars ('I thought that if you had an acoustic guitar / Then it meant that you were a protest singer / Oh, I can smile about it now, but at the time it was terrible'). The song actually has a piano as its lead instrument, which was a first for The Smiths at this point, being also one of the first songs Marr ever wrote on a piano, and Rourke also managed to play a bit of cello in the background as well. The cover star of the single was actor Pat Phoenix, best known for her iconic role as Elsie Tanner in the long-running ITV soap *Coronation Street*.

'What She Said' (Morrissey/Marr)

(see *Meat Is Murder* album)

'Stretch Out and Wait' (Morrissey/Marr)

This song is actually available in two slightly different versions. The one released on this single was later available on the *Louder Than Bombs* compilation and had slightly different lyrics than the version released on the *The World Won't Listen* compilation. Musically, it's a breezy and light tune, where Joyce is playing the drums with brushes, and Rourke adds his intricate bass lines, as usual. In the lyrics, Morrissey borrowed a line from the brilliant Australian band The Go-Betweens, who released two singles on Rough Trade in 1982 and 1983. On their debut single, 'Karen', Robert Forster sings 'Cause the girls that I see / Walking around, yeah the ones I see / Walking on the street / Are so damn-da-da-da-damned cold / 'Cos they must have Eskimo blood in their veins'.

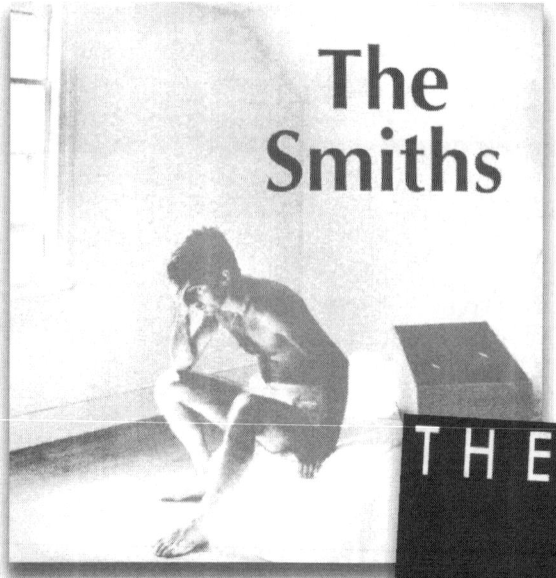

Left: The cover for the 'William It Was Really Nothing' single, a number 17 hit released in August 1984. (*Rough Trade*)

Right: 'How Soon is Now', not a major hit but one of the band's most enduring songs. Cover star: Sean Barrett from the 1958 movie *Dunkirk*. (*Rough Trade*)

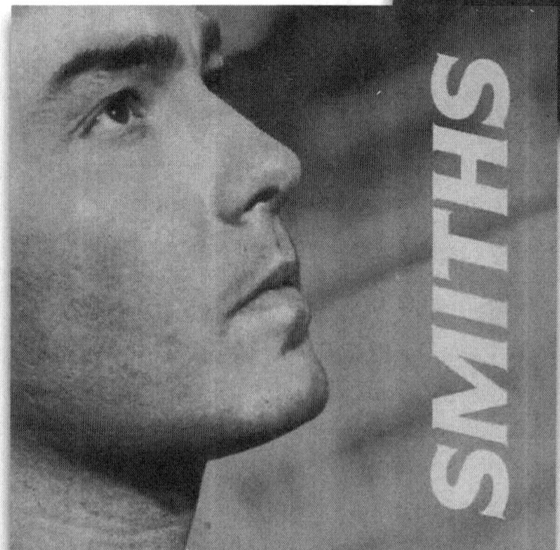

Left: 'Panic' released in July 1986, featuring cover star Richard Bradford, star of 1960s series *Man in a Suitcase*. (*Rough Trade*)

Right: 'Ask', a number 14 hit in the UK released in October 1986. Cover star: Yootha Joyce. (*Rough Trade*)

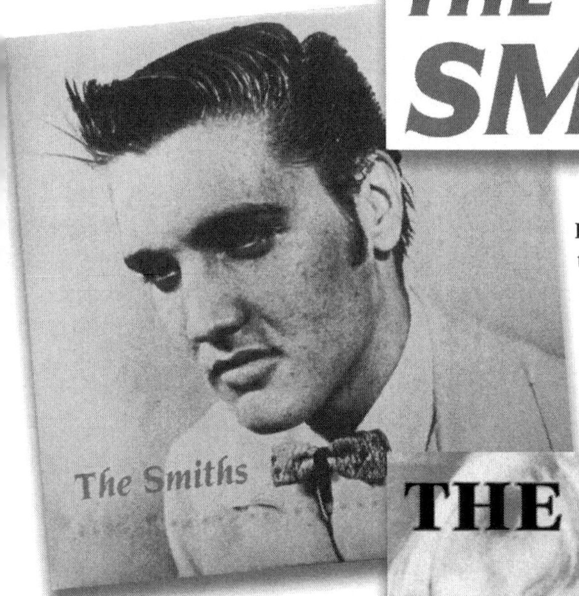

Left: The 'Shoplifters of the World Unite' single, released in January 1987 and featuring Elvis Presley on the picture sleeve. (*Rough Trade*)

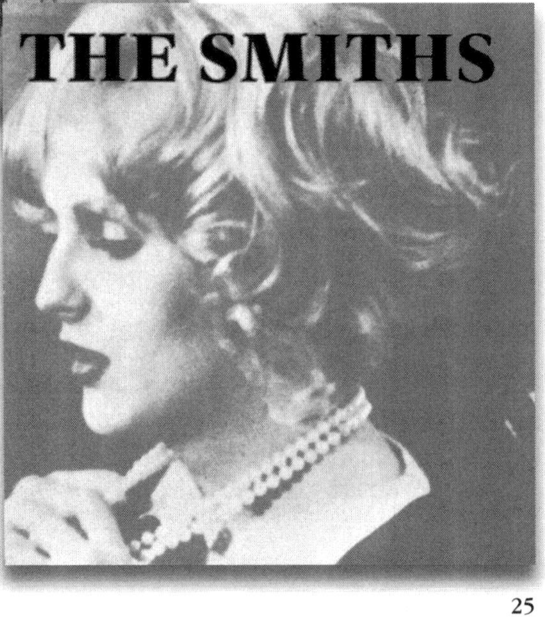

Right: 'Sheila Take a Bow' was the last stand alone single recorded by the band, released in April 1987. Cover star: Candy Darling. (*Rough Trade*)

The Queen Is Dead (1986)

Personnel:
Morrissey: vocals
Johnny Marr: guitars, orchestration, synthesized strings, harmonium, marimba
Andy Rourke: bass guitar
Mike Joyce: drums, tambourine
Caryn Gough: layout
Morrissey: sleeve
Alain Delon: cover star (photo taken from the 1964 movie 'L'Insoumis')
Steve Wright: group photo
Toshi Yajima: Morrissey photo
Recorded at RAK Studios (London), Jacob Studios (Farnham) and Wessex Studios (London)
Produced by Morrissey and Johnny Marr
Playing time: 36:48
Label: Rough Trade (UK), Sire (US)
Release date: June 16th 1986
Highest chart position: UK: 2, US: 70

What many regards as The Smiths' masterpiece, was mainly written by Johnny Marr while the band was on tour in support of the *Meat Is Murder* album in 1985. During soundchecks, he played his new compositions to Rourke and Joyce, and together they arranged the songs before Morrissey provided the lyrics to them.

It's probably no exaggeration to say that *The Queen Is Dead* is the band's most famous album in this day and age. In 2013, music magazine *NME* voted the album 'the greatest album of all time', placing it higher than classic records by The Beatles and David Bowie, for instance.

This time, the production is credited to just Morrissey and Marr (unlike *Meat Is Murder*, where the whole band were credited as producers), with Stephen Street once again handling the engineering. When talking to the magazine *Sound On Sound* in 2005, Street said that the recording sessions were very constructive and that he, Morrissey and Marr had a really good working relationship, as they were more or less the same age and had the same reference points.

The band began recording the album in the summer of 1985 when they recorded a demo for the upcoming single 'The boy with the Thorn in his Side'. The demo was then deemed good enough for release, and the single eventually came out in September that year. The rest of the album was recorded during winter 1985-1986, and it originally had the working title 'Margaret On The Guillotine' (which would be the title of a song on Morrissey's debut solo album, *Viva Hate*, in 1988), but the band eventually settled for *The Queen Is Dead*, which was just as controversial, as the working title.

At a quick glance, it might appear that things were constantly coming up roses for The Smiths at this time, but it was actually rather the opposite. The band were having a lengthy dispute with their label, and troublesome negotiations regarding their contract meant that the release of the album was postponed for many months. Then in February 1986, after coming home from a tour of Ireland, Andy Rourke was kicked out of the band because of his growing drug addiction. He was replaced by Craig Gannon (former member of Aztec Camera and The Bluebells), but Rourke was soon asked to join the band again, and Gannon became The Smiths' rhythm guitarist instead, playing with them for a couple of singles, and on the tour following *The Queen Is Dead*. Their singles were selling less in the UK, and some people believed that The Smiths were on their way out. The band were soon about to prove them wrong.

'The Queen Is Dead' (Morrissey/Marr)

The album opener is also its title track, and it's one hell of a powerful start. After a snippet taken from the movie *The L-Shaped Room* from 1962, where Cicely Courtneidge sings 'Take me back to dear Old Blighty', Mike Joyce enters with the now-classic tom-tom intro (which was actually created by Joyce and Stephen Street using a sampler), and soon the rest of the band clashes in and joins him in this song about anti-royalty. It's a song without a chorus, and the dominating ingredients in the soundscape are Marr's wah-wah guitar and Rourke's intricate bass lines (as always). Lyrically, Morrissey is undoubtedly mocking the British royal family once again, but he's also singing about having a chat with the Queen (after breaking into her castle), and about Prince Charles dressing up in his mother's bridal veil. It's far from their best song, but it's still important in The Smiths canon.

'Frankly, Mr Shankly' (Morrissey/Marr)

So we go from a song about wanting to see the Queen dead, to a song that's allegedly about Rough Trade boss Geoff Travis (who did indeed write poetry) – although it has also been suggested that the song is about Morrissey himself and his status in the contemporary pop scene. The song is very jaunty, kind of resembling a German oom-pah tune in its verse (it was indeed originally meant to be a 'homage' to Sandie Shaw's Eurovision winner 'Puppet on a String'), which combines well with Morrissey's satirical and cynical lyrics. As you may have noticed in the credits for the album, this is the only song not engineered by Street. This is because the tape with the original recording was discovered to be faulty, so the band had to re-record the song with former producer John Porter just in time for the album's final mix.

'I Know It's Over' (Morrissey/Marr)

There has always been a popular opinion among non-Smiths fans that Morrissey is a depressing guy, and that view is largely founded on this album, with this song being one of the reasons. From its opening lines: 'Oh mother, I can feel the soil falling over my head / And as I climb into an empty bed / Oh well, enough said,' it just keeps getting bleaker and bleaker, until the desperate wailing during the coda. Actually, it strikes me what a journey Morrissey had made as a singer in just a couple of years – compare the growling and yelping on the debut album to the crooning on *The Queen Is Dead*, for instance. That's not saying that he was a poor singer on those first recordings, not at all, just a different kind of vocalist. 'I Know It's Over' also contains one of the most cited Morrissey lines: 'It's so easy to laugh / It's so easy to hate / It takes guts to be gentle and kind.'

'Never Had No One Ever' (Morrissey/Marr)
Well, the title says it all, doesn't it? Yes, it's another one of those 'depressing' Morrissey songs, and this one is just as dark as the song before it. In the song, Morrissey mentions that he had a bad dream that lasted '20 years, 7 months and 28 days'. According to biographer Johnny Rogan, Morrissey's journal for the day in question (January 18th, 1980) shows that he was reading the book *The Murderer's Who's Who*, and complaining about a sore foot, which doesn't really sound like something that would end a bad dream to me. Actually, Morrissey said to *Melody Maker* in 1986 that the song was about him not feeling at home in Manchester.

'Cemetry Gates' (Morrissey/Marr)
Morrissey never hid his sources of inspiration and his idols–from putting them on the record sleeves, to 'stealing' bits and pieces for his lyrics. In this song, he also gets to name drop a few of them (like Oscar Wilde, John Keats, and William Yeats), whilst contemplating how fragile life is as he walks through a cemetery (Morrissey used to take walks on the Southern Cemetery in Manchester when he was young). Ironically, in a song where he talks about plagiarism ('If you must write prose and poems / The words you use should be your own / Don't plagiarise or take 'on loan'), he did indeed 'borrow' a bunch of lines from the movie *The Man Who Came to Dinner* (1942). And have you noticed that the word 'cemetery' is misspelt in the title? According to Morrissey, he always had a problem spelling the word and mistakenly spelt it incorrectly in the song title. Musically, the acoustic arrangement by Marr is light and beautiful and complements Morrissey's rather bright lyrics in an excellent way.

'Bigmouth Strikes Again' (Morrissey/Marr)
Johnny Marr told *Guitar Player* magazine that he wrote this song with the intention of making a 'Jumpin' Jack Flash' for The Smiths, and I guess he succeeded in that. He also insisted that this would be the first single to be released off the album, instead of 'There Is a Light That Never Goes Out', which the label preferred, and with hindsight, he was probably right about that too. This is a real pop smash, with Morrissey shouting back at the media of the

time, and also picturing himself as a martyr, comparing his struggles to those of Joan of Arc. The 'female' backing vocals are credited to Ann Coates, but it is actually Morrissey's voice sped up (Rourke told the *NME* that the vocalist had a hard time recording the backing vocals, as he kept breaking up in fits of laughter all the time), and the name is a play on the Manchester area 'Ancoats'. Nowadays, Morrissey has replaced the reference to a Walkman melting to it being an iPod instead when playing the song live.

'The Boy With the Thorn in His Side' (Morrissey/Marr)

The first song recorded for the album was also the first teaser, released as a single in September 1985. Lyric wise, this is yet another song where Morrissey is attacking those who have mistreated him. This time it's the music business, which he claims is the 'thorn', but he is also explaining his outspoken and controversial public persona with a longing for love. Unusually for The Smiths, the single was accompanied by a music video, something that the band had tried to avoid as much as they could. Marr later told *Q Magazine* that he thought the video was 'utterly crap' and that they only did it to please their label. The cover star of the single was US author Truman Capote, a photo taken by Cecil Beaton in the late 40s.

'Vicar in a Tutu' (Morrissey/Marr)

Keeping in the rockabilly tradition started on the previous album, Marr arranged this song as a real rockabilly rocker. Mike Joyce told author Johnny Rogan that the song grew out of a studio jam, where Marr began playing the main guitar riff and Joyce then added his drums on top of it. Lyrically, the song is quite clearly a satirical view of a priest with transvestite leanings, and he also tells the world that they should not judge him for that: 'The vicar in a tutu / He's not strange / He just wants to live his life this way.'

'There Is a Light That Never Goes Out' (Morrissey/Marr)

When talking about the most famous Smiths songs, I think it's basically down to three: 'This Charming Man', 'How Soon Is Now?', and of course, 'There Is a Light That Never Goes Out'. This is Morrissey's grand love song, featuring the immoral lines: 'And if a double-decker bus / Crashes into us / To die by your side / Is such a heavenly way to die.' In the lyrics, Morrissey pictures himself riding along with a very dear friend in his or her car and would rather just keep on driving than be dropped off at home. Musically, the song is more or less a very straightforward pop song, but with the added twist of a string section. Or, that's what they want us to think. On the sleeve, the strings are credited to The Hated Salford Ensemble, which is more or less Johnny Marr and a synthesizer. He also added the synth flute (which was originally meant to be played on the guitar). In an interview with *NME* in 2011, Morrissey talked about the recording session and said that it was magical, that the band really felt they had recorded something special. He also added that if you crank the volume up, you can supposedly hear him say 'that was amazing!' at the end of the song. Well, I haven't found it yet, but I'm sure someone will. The song was never released as a single in the UK in the band's lifetime (even though it was supposed to be the first single off the album) but got the 7' and CD single treatment when Warner Brothers started their re-release campaign in 1992, peaking at #25 in the UK.

'Some Girls Are Bigger Than Others' (Morrissey/Marr)

This closing track has one of the weirdest intros ever, as the song fades in, then quickly fades out, and finally fades back in again. According to Marr, he wanted the effect of a door closing and opening, but I'm not sure if they nailed that, to be honest. The song itself, however, is brilliant, with an amazing jangly guitar line from Marr throughout the tune. And if songs like 'I Know It's Over' showed Morrissey's more depressing and dark side, this song is proof as good as any that he had a lot of humour as well. He ends the song with the line: 'Send me the pillow / The one that you dream on,' which is borrowed from Johnny Tillotson's hit single 'Send Me The Pillow You Dream On' from 1962. What a way to end a smashing album!

Contemporary Singles

Panic (single, 1986)

Personnel:
Morrissey: vocals
Johnny Marr: guitars, piano
Craig Gannon: guitars
Andy Rourke: bass guitar, cello
Mike Joyce: drums

'Panic' (Morrissey/Marr)

Probably one of the better-known songs in The Smiths' catalogue, it was released as a single on July 21st 1986 and peaked at #11 on the UK singles chart. This was the first song they recorded after Rourke was kicked out and then asked to join again, and his replacement Craig Gannon is heard playing the rhythm guitar for the first time here. The inspiration for the lyrics came, famously, after Morrissey and Marr listened to the radio news reports when the nuclear disaster in Chernobyl occurred in April 1986, where the DJ Steve Wright chose to play Wham!'s jaunty hit 'I'm Your Man' directly after the report of this horrendous accident, which upset the two songwriters. Morrissey later wore a t-shirt with a photo of Wright and the words 'Hang The DJ!' on stage. There was also some controversy after the music press misinterpreted the line 'burn down the disco' as an attack on black music, but Marr soon came to Morrissey's defence in the *NME*, saying that 'it makes no earthly sense'. The cover star for the single was the American actor Richard Bradford (best known for the 60s thriller series *Man in a Suitcase*). Morrissey has later claimed that this is his favourite Smiths song.

'Vicar in a Tutu' (Morrissey/Marr)
(see *The Queen Is Dead* album)

'The Draize Train' (Marr)
One of the three instrumental songs that the band released, and this one was written by Marr alone (as opposed to 'Oscillate Wildly', where Morrissey is listed as joint songwriter). Label boss Geoff Travis really wanted Moz to write some lyrics for this funky song, as he felt that it could be a huge hit, but the singer felt that it was one of the weakest songs Marr had written so far, so he declined. Instead, the band recorded this one without their singer, but Moz apparently liked it enough to allow his bandmates to play it live – maybe he liked to have a few minutes rest during the show – and a live rendition can be heard on the *Rank* live album.

Ask (single, 1986)

Personnel:
Morrissey: vocals
Johnny Marr: guitars
Craig Gannon: guitars
Andy Rourke: bass guitar
Mike Joyce: drums

'Ask' (Morrissey/Marr)
Before releasing an album full of long song titles, the band came out with two singles in a row with just one word in their title, this being the second one, after 'Panic'. It was released on October 20th 1986 but didn't fare as well as the previous effort, peaking at #14 in the UK singles chart (though it did make it to the top ten in Ireland!) With 'Panic' being the protest song it was, Morrissey deliberately wrote non-protest lyrics for this one, to make sure that the fans wouldn't get tired of them. Instead he suggested that you should break free of your inhibitions, and stop being shy (which of course is easier said than done for some). He also mentions 'the bomb that will bring us together', which could be connected to the famous line in the future solo single 'Everyday Is Like Sunday' ('come, come, nuclear bomb!'), but this is reportedly rather about sexual desire, which is more fitting with the song's overall theme. The female backing vocals were provided by Kirsty MacColl (who had a bunch of hits on her own in the UK in the 80s and 90s, before her tragic death in a speedboat accident in Mexico in December 2000, at just 41 years old). And as it was a Smiths song, there was also some controversy surrounding the release of the single. Firstly, guitarist Gannon claimed he helped write the song, but didn't get any writing credit, and then Morrissey decided to let MacColl's husband, producer Steve Lillywhite, remix the track that John Porter recorded, which enraged the latter, as he had grand plans for the track that never became reality.

The cover star on the single was the actor Yootha Joyce (no relation to Mike), a character actor on TV and film in the 1960s but best known for the 70s sitcom *Man About the House*.

'Cemetry Gates' (Morrissey/Marr)
(see *The Queen Is Dead* album)

'Golden Lights' (Lynn Ripley)
I think it's fair to say that this might be one of the most 'hated' Smiths recordings, and it does stand out a bit from their other efforts. It was the first cover version the band released, with the original being recorded by Twinkle in 1965. The backing vocals were once again provided by Kirsty MacColl, and Morrissey sounds like he's singing underwater with all the strange effects that were added into the mix. It's probably not a wild guess that this was one of the songs that made Marr doubt why he was still in the band …

Shoplifters of the World Unite (single, 1987)

Personnel:
Morrissey: vocals
Johnny Marr: guitars
Craig Gannon: guitars
Andy Rourke: bass guitar
Mike Joyce: drums

'Shoplifters of the World Unite' (Morrissey/Marr)
Released as The Smiths' thirteenth single on January 26th 1987 (peaking at #12 in the UK), it replaced 'You Just Haven't Earned It Yet, Baby' as the planned A-side (the label even pressed 900 copies before they changed their mind). It might sound like a hymn to thievery, but I don't think you should take the lyrics literally, as it's probably 'a metaphor for all those repressed and marginalised by society', as author Simon Goddard wrote in his book *Mozipedia* (2009). Morrissey himself has also said that the song is about 'spiritual shoplifting'. Apart from that, the lyrics appear to be filled with 'loans' from other works, like *The Last Chance Texaco* (Rickie Lee Jones, 1979), *Don Juan's Reckless Daughter* (Joni Mitchell, 1977), and a snippet from a James Dean TV drama from 1952 called *Campbell Playhouse*. This is the only song in The Smiths catalogue that was produced by only Johnny Marr, just shortly after he was involved in a serious car crash in November 1986. The cover star of the single is Elvis Presley, who, I guess, doesn't need any further introduction.

'Half a Person' (Morrissey/Marr)
This was one of the first songs I ever heard by The Smiths, and probably the one that made me fall in love with the band in the mid-90s. It forms some

kind of trilogy with 'London' and 'Is It Really So Strange?', as they're all about moving from the north to the south (Manchester to London, for instance). Marr has said that it's one of his favourite among the songs he wrote with Morrissey. He remembers the exact moment that they wrote it, on the stairway to the Mayfair Studio, and that it was probably the best songwriting moment the two ever shared. You can almost feel that moment in the song, as well. The narrator of the song says that he's '16, clumsy and shy', and in his autobiography, Morrissey mentions that he moved to London for a few days when he was seventeen. What other band could hide away a song of this quality on a B-side?

'London' (Morrissey/Marr)

Probably the hardest rocking song in The Smiths canon. The lyrics are about a man who boards a train to Euston, leaving his dismal hometown behind while sneering at the people staying up north – a theme he borrowed from the book *By Grand Central Station I Saw Down And Wept* by Elizabeth Smart (which also contains the sentence 'because you notice the jealousy of those that stay at home', a line that's remarkably similar to Morrissey's: 'but did you see jealousy in the eyes of the ones who had to stay behind?' The lead guitar during the song's chaotic coda was played by Craig Gannon.

Sheila Take a Bow (single, 1987)

Personnel:
Morrissey: vocals
Johnny Marr: guitars
Andy Rourke: bass guitar
Mike Joyce: drums

'Sheila Take a Bow' (Morrissey/Marr)

Released as the band's 14th single on April 13th 1987, the song was originally planned to feature Sandie Shaw on backing vocals. She recorded her vocal track (after Morrissey sang her the tune on the phone, as he was at home sick when Sandie came to the studio), but in the end, the band opted not to use her vocal. Shaw later claimed that the song was 'horrid', so it was probably for the best, then. Once again, the band scrapped an original John Porter recording in favour of a Stephen Street version. The single eventually peaked at #10 in the UK singles charts, matching 'Heaven Knows I'm Miserable Now' as their best-selling single. The song has quite a lot in common with the UK glam rock scene of the 70s, and Marr has admitted that he was trying to find a 'Mott the Hoople sound' for the tune. Lyrically, the lines 'Throw your homework onto the fire' probably inspired one or two young Smiths fans to rebel against their parents.The cover star for the single was transgender actor Candy Darling, a photo taken while shooting *Women in Revolt* (1971).

'Is It Really So Strange?' (Morrissey/Marr)

One of the three songs that make up Morrissey's 'moving from the north to the south' trilogy (the other parts being 'London' and 'Half a Person'). It was originally recorded for the B-side of 'Ask' in June 1986, but the band weren't happy with the recording, so the version of the song that was later released on this single was taken from their last Peel session in late 1986. Of the three trilogy songs, this is by far the most humorous one, as Morrissey tells his tale of chasing his love interest all over the UK, and during his travels, he kills both a nun and a horse, for some reason. Musically, it's yet another of the rockabilly influenced songs that the band recorded, though this is one of the slower ones.

'Sweet and Tender Hooligan' (Morrissey/Marr)

One of the few Smiths rockers, 'Sweet and Tender Hooligan' was initially recorded for the 'Panic' single, but just as with 'Is It Really So Strange?', the band deemed the recording not good enough (they thought they played the song too slowly). Instead, they tried it again when they went to John Peel for the last time, in December 1986, and this time they nailed it. That version was eventually released on this B-side, and would finally be promoted to being an A-side when Sire decided to release an EP of rare tracks (instead of 'Ask', which was released by WEA in Europe) in the US, in support of the *Singles* compilation of 1995. Lyrically, Morrissey tells the tale of a young criminal in court, who swears that he'd 'never never do it again'. Towards the end of the song, Morrissey throws in a twist on the expression 'in the midst of life we are in death', turning it into 'in the midst of life we are in debt'.

Strangeways, Here We Come (1987)

Personnel:
Morrissey: vocals, piano, handclaps
Johnny Marr: guitar, keyboards, harmonica, harmonium, autoharp, synthesizer strings, saxophone arrangement, additional vocals (on 'Death at One's Elbow'), handclaps, production
Andy Rourke: bass guitar, keyboards, handclaps
Mike Joyce: drums, tambourine, handclaps
Stephen Street: drum machine programming, string arrangements, sound effects
Caryn Gough: layout
Morrissey: sleeve
Richard Davalos: cover star (photo taken from the 1965 movie 'East of Eden')
Recorded at The Wool Hall (Beckington, Somerset)
Produced by Morrissey, Johnny Marr and Stephen Street
Playing time: 36:37
Label: Rough Trade (UK), Sire (US)
Release date: September 28th 1987
Highest chart position: UK: 2, US: 55

After striving for international success for a few years, The Smiths finally had a hit album with *The Queen Is Dead*, a record that also gave them something of a breakthrough in the US as well. Now the path was cleared in front of them, and they were off to international stardom, with arena gigs and extensive media coverage. One of the things that had held them back from all this, according to the band, was their deal with indie label Rough Trade (even though they were signed to major label Sire in the US), so while continuing to renegotiate that deal, the band recorded what would become their last studio album, *Strangeways, Here We Come*.

Before the band entered the Wool Hall studio (then owned by pop stars Tears for Fears), they got rid of Craig Gannon, and also asked Stephen Street to help them with the recordings once again, this time as a credited co-producer (with Morrissey and Marr). The sessions are now mostly (in)famous for the after-work parties, with the well-kept wine cellar in the studio premises one of the main reasons for the extensive partying (though they started drinking after Morrissey had gone to bed, as he didn't want anything to do with those sorts of things, according to Street).

Both Morrissey and Marr have later said that this is their favourite among the band's four albums, and while I don't agree with them, it certainly has some magical moments. To call it The Smiths' most diverse album isn't an exaggeration. If the band had used synthesizers and keyboards as an experiment on *The Queen Is Dead*, they had now fully embraced them and made this an integral part of the soundscape. Of course, this upset a lot of the band's fans, as they saw The Smiths as a guitar pop band, but Marr, in particular, felt that they had to develop as a band, and break free from their shackles of jangly indie-pop if they wanted to get anywhere.

During the time from the recording of the album in March and April 1987, to its release in September that same year, the band broke up. When Marr told the rest of the band that he was leaving, *Strangeways, Here We Come* was released posthumously, and therefore most of the songs on the album were never played live by the band– they played their last gig together in Italy in February 1987. And by the way – Strangeways is a Manchester prison.

'A Rush and a Push and the Land Is Ours' (Morrissey/Marr)

While the song itself might not go down in Smiths history as their most memorable, it does hold a very special place in their catalogue – it's the only song they ever recorded with no guitars at all, which must be seen as a bit odd for a band with one of the world's most renowned guitarists in its lineup. But this was all part of Marr's desire to further develop the band's sound. Lyrically, the song is one of many on this album that deals with death in one form or another, and it all kicks off with Morrissey presenting himself as 'the ghost of Troubled Joe', who, in the song, hung eighteen months earlier.

'I Started Something I Couldn't Finish' (Morrissey/Marr)

Released as the second single taken from the album in November 1987 (peaking at #23 in the UK), the song begins with a few power chords from Marr, and then goes on to reveal details about a fictional (?) relationship that Morrissey doesn't seem to be too convinced about. It wasn't originally planned for a single release, but the label felt that it was inappropriate to put 'Stop Me if You Think You've Heard This One Before' on a 7', as it mentions planning a mass murder, and the Hungerford massacre (where Michael Ryan shot and killed sixteen people in a small town in Berkshire, England) had taken place just a few months earlier. The video that was shot for the 'Stop me…' release, showing Morrissey riding on a bike through Manchester together with a bunch of lookalike fans, was then used for this release instead (though it was later included on future video releases as the video for 'Stop me…'). At the end of the song, Morrissey can be heard talking to producer Street: 'OK Stephen, shall we do that again?'

'Death of a Disco Dancer' (Morrissey/Marr)

Hardly a fan favourite, this song offers quite a pessimistic view on world peace in our lifetime: 'And if you think peace is a common goal / Well, that goes to show how little you know,' and 'Love, peace and harmony? /... / Very nice, very nice, very nice / But maybe in the next world'. This song is also unique in its own way, as it's the first and only time Morrissey played an instrument on a Smiths recording, though I'm not sure his tinkering on the piano in the coda of the song can be labelled 'playing'.

'Girlfriend in a Coma' (Morrissey/Marr)

The first song released from the album as a single, in August 1987, peaking at #13 in the UK singles charts. The single's two B-side tracks were also the last songs the band ever recorded together (the Cilla Black cover 'Work Is a Four-Letter Word' and 'I Keep Mine Hidden') in a session that has been described by most of those attending it as 'horrible', as the band was on the verge of breaking up at this point. On the single's picture sleeve, Shelagh Delaney made yet another appearance in The Smiths history, this time as the cover star. And as the band suddenly allowed music videos to be made, with this one featuring Morrissey miming to the song over footage from the movie *The Leather Boys* (1964). This song is actually about a girlfriend (it remains unclear who's girlfriend it is) being in a coma, and Morrissey seems unsure whether he thinks it's a good thing or a bad thing, even though he says that he 'would hate anything to happen to her'.

'Stop Me if You Think You've Heard This One Before' (Morrissey/Marr)

Yet another long song title (there are several on this album) which was seen by some as a sign of self-parody when it was released – but the lyrics are not about Morrissey being repetitive. Instead, he sings about a relationship in its final stages, during which the narrator drinks too much and has a minor cycling 'accident'. As already mentioned, the mentioning of a mass murder made the band stop the release of a single containing the song in the UK, but it did come out in several other countries. If you have a secret wish to be like Morrissey for a few minutes, you can sing 'Stop me...' if you happen to own the *Rock Band 3* video game.

'Last Night I Dreamt That Somebody Loved Me' (Morrissey/Marr)

The long intro (which consists of a BBC sound recording from the miners' strike in 1984-1985 and some maudlin piano) immediately sets the mood for this song, and after almost two minutes, it breaks into a dramatic tune, in which Morrissey is once again longing for love, the drama intensified by Marr's synthesizer string arrangement (this time credited to Orchestrazia Ardwick). The song was also released as the last single during the band's lifetime (although they had split more than six months before it came out in December 1987), and on the 7', the long intro was omitted, which made the song finish after a mere three minutes (the album version was released on the 12', though). The cover star was the British singer Billy Fury, whose song 'Don't Jump' inspired the lyrics to the song 'Shakespeare's Sister'.

'Unhappy Birthday' (Morrissey/Marr)

As ever so often with Smiths songs, Marr's fairly happy music once again contrasts with Morrissey's rather nasty birthday wishes for – well, we don't know who he had in mind here, but one thing is for sure – it's not his best friend. The lines 'I've come to wish you an unhappy birthday / 'Cause you're evil and you lie / And if you should die / I may feel slightly sad / But I won't cry' tell the story straight. Marr once said that this was one of his favourite Smiths songs, partly because of the amazing interplay between his guitar and Rourke's bass: 'Only we could play it, and only Morrissey could sing it.' I think he's quite right about that.

'Paint a Vulgar Picture' (Morrissey/Marr)

That the band had some issues with their label, Rough Trade, was not a secret back in those days, and this song really tells it as they saw it. Morrissey tells the story of a greedy record label who has a dead star in its roster who continue to exploit his back catalogue with endless reissuing and repackaging. But amid all this label heckling, he also finds the time to tell the story of a big fan, 'a child from those ugly new houses', who dreams of meeting his big idol. That the lyrics were aimed at Rough Trade boss Geoff Travis were made even more clear when Morrissey included one of Travis' favourite sayings, 'you just haven't earned it yet, baby' (which was also the title of a Smiths song). Since the demise of The Smiths, the lyrics have become more and more ironic, as Warner keeps releasing compilation after compilation of the band's back catalogue. Incidentally, this was one of the first Smiths songs Morrissey played live as a solo artist in the late 90s, after years of refusing to play those old songs.

'Death at One's Elbow' (Morrissey/Marr)

Did I mention that death was a theme for this album? Well, this title makes it all too clear, really. Also, it's rockabilly time again! The title of the song was taken from the diaries of Joe Orton (the full quote is: 'As the corpse is downstairs in the main living room, it means going out or watching television with death at one's elbow,' with the corpse in question being his mother, whose funeral he attended the same day), and the lyrics also echo Orton's own demise, as he was beaten to death by his lover in August 1967. I think it's fair to say that this is yet another one of those songs that's hardly any fan's favourite, but it does mark another first in The Smiths history (at least to my knowledge), as Marr provides the backing vocals.

'I Won't Share You' (Morrissey/Marr)

The last song of the last Smiths album – and it's a very fitting closer, with its lullaby-like tune. Ever since The Smiths split up, there have been vivid speculations on the reasons why the band chose to part ways, and one of the more frequent ones is that Morrissey was annoyed with Marr 'moonlighting' with other artists (like Kirsty MacColl and Pretenders), and that he would prefer the guitarist to focus on his own band instead. With that in mind, the lyrics to this song become almost self-explanatory. Marr told author Simon Goddard in May 2004 that if the lyrics were aimed at him, he would feel quite good about it and that it's a nice song.

Other Contemporary Songs

'What's the World' (Jim Glennie/Paul Gilbertson/Gavan Whelan/Tim Booth)

During their tour of Scotland in the autumn of 1985, The Smiths added this song, taken from James' debut EP 'Jimone' (released on Factory Records in 1983), to their setlist, mostly to add a slightly different dynamic to their shows, according to Marr. When it was time to release the 'I Started Something I Couldn't Finish' single in November 1987, a live recording from the gig in Glasgow in September 1985 was added to the cassette single, despite the fact that the recording originally wasn't meant to be released.

'I Keep Mine Hidden' (Morrissey/Marr)

This B-side to 'Girlfriend in a Coma' was the last song that Morrissey and Marr ever recorded together, and you really wish that such an amazing songwriting partnership could have ended on a higher note than this whistling, jolly tune. To put it short – this is as far from a classic Smiths song that they ever go. During the same studio session (with producer Grant Showbiz), the band also recorded the much-hated cover of Cilla Black's 'Work Is a Four-Letter Word' (which ended up on the same single), and a rendition of the Elvis Presley hit single 'A Fool Such As I' (a cover that is yet to be released). In the lyrics, Morrissey sings about how hard he finds it to express his emotions, and also how he envies those who can.

'Work Is a Four-Letter Word' (Guy Woolfenden/Don Black)

Together with the previous song, 'I Keep Mine Hidden', this was the last song the band ever recorded together, and most fans seem to think that those two are the worst recordings they ever put out. And it's hard to disagree, really. This cover of Cilla Black's 1968 recording (which was available on the B-side of 'Where Is Tomorrow?') came out on the 'Girlfriend in a Coma' single, and Marr later said in interviews that it was the last straw for him, and shortly after the sessions, he decided to leave the band.

Smiths Compilations

Normally, a band's output of compilations isn't interesting in a context like this, as they almost always consist of songs available on the regular albums. But The Smiths catalogue is different. The second album they released, after the self-titled debut, was the compilation *Hatful of Hollow* in November 1984, which was made up of the non-album singles released so far, BBC live sessions and B-sides. They kept with this tradition later on with *The World Won't Listen* (1987), compiling the same kind of material from 1985 to 1987, and also *Louder Than Bombs* (1987), which was originally intended for the US, but was later released in the UK as well.

Since then, there have been a handful of additional Smiths compilations released, most notably *Best...I* and *Best...II*, released in 1992 when Warner bought the band's back catalogue, and later, *Singles* (1995) and *The Sound of The Smiths* (2008, available as both single and double disc). In 2008, Rhino Records released *The Smiths Singles Box*, containing re-pressings of the first ten 7' singles released in the UK between 1983 and 1986, plus the rare Dutch only 7' release of 'The Headmaster Ritual' and the promo only 7' of 'Still Ill'. The CD version of this box set also contained the songs from the 12' versions of the singles, which meant that there were a lot more songs on the digital release.

A few years later, Rhino also released the *Complete* box set, which contained all the original albums, the live album *Rank*, and the three compilations released in the 80s. The albums were all remastered, with Marr being highly involved in the mastering process.

Considering Morrissey's harsh comments on the greedy labels in 'Paint a Vulgar Picture', one could say that maybe he was just being prophetic.

In the following sections, I will deal with the original 80s compilations listed above. As some of the songs appear on the studio albums (although in different versions), I will focus on the non-album songs here, with just a short description of the differences between where songs we've already discussed, differ.

Hatful of Hollow (compilation, 1984)

Caryn Gough: layout
Morrissey: sleeve
Fabrice Colette: cover star
Playing time: 56:11
Label: Rough Trade (UK), Sire (US)
Release date: November 12th 1984
Highest chart position: UK: 7

When *Hatful of Hollow* was released, not even nine months after the debut album came out, it was quite a risky project. That a band compiled it themselves after just one album and a couple of singles, was unique, and a major label (as opposed to an indie) would probably have stopped the band from going forward with it. But Rough Trade gave in to Morrissey's idea, as he felt that the songs they had recorded for their BBC sessions represented the band much better than the murky sound of the first album – the sessions capturing the band's energetic live performances in a more accurate way.

At the time of its release in 1984, the compilation was sold at mid-price (maximum £3.99), and as the total playing time was almost an hour, this was a real bargain and a perfect introduction to the band for the sceptics. When reading about how fans of the band discovered them, many people say that this album was the one that got them into The Smiths, which proves that Morrissey's hunch was probably right.

The original sleeve art contained the photo of Fabrice Colette, taken from a French newspaper in 1983, a blue frame with 'The Smiths' printed above the photo, and the album title in a 'ribbon' in the lower part. However, after 1987, the frame was deleted and the sleeve just consisted of the Colette photo, with the names superimposed on the picture. The original sleeve design did make a comeback on the reissue in 2011, though.

'William, It Was Really Nothing' (Morrissey/Marr)

(see 'William, It Was Really Nothing' single)

'What Difference Does It Make?' (Morrissey/Marr)

This is the version the band recorded for the Peel session on May 31 1983, and it's widely considered to be far superior to the one that they recorded for the album with John Porter. The biggest difference is probably in the drumming, which is far more energetic and aggressive, and the bass, which is far more audible here. This version has also been used on many of the posthumous single's compilations, demonstrating that the band really preferred this recording.

'These Things Take Time' (Morrissey/Marr)

Recorded for the first David Jensen session on July 4 1983, this is another one of Morrissey's lyrics about wanting love and never seeming to obtain it.

The song was originally featured on the B-side on the 12' version of 'What Difference Does It Make?', and the differences between the two versions are almost exactly the same as with the aforementioned song – more energetic drumming and a more audible bass.

'This Charming Man' (Morrissey/Marr)
This song was originally written for the Peel session the band recorded on September 21 1983, and that's the version included here. The first difference you will hear when listening to it is that Marr's famous intro is missing, and also that the whole song is a lot softer than the version we are used to from the 7' single (and the debut album if you have a version that contains this song). More on the song under the 'This Charming Man' single.

'Handsome Devil' (Morrissey/Marr)
(see 'Hand in Glove' single)

'Hand in Glove' (Morrissey/Marr)
(see 'Hand in Glove' single)

'Still Ill' (Morrissey/Marr)
Another song from the debut album, this version was recorded for the Peel session in September 1983. The main difference compared to the album version is Marr's harmonica during the intro and outro of the song, but it's also a bit slower, so you get the impression that the band sounds a bit unenthusiastic when playing it. I hope they weren't.

'Heaven Knows I'm Miserable Now' (Morrissey/Marr)
(see 'Heaven Knows I'm Miserable Now' single)

'This Night Has Opened My Eyes' (Morrissey/Marr)
Recorded for the September 1983 session for John Peel, this song has only been officially released in this version, even though there's supposed to be a regular studio version hidden away somewhere (recorded in the summer of 1984 with John Porter) – it was meant to be released as the B-side to the 'Nowhere Fast' single that never came to be. This was also the only song on the compilation that hadn't been released in any form up until now. Lyrically, this more or less tells the story of the play, and later movie, *A Taste of Honey* by Shelagh Delaney, rewritten into a three minute and 41-second pop song, with Morrissey even taking the liberty of borrowing a few lines directly from the script. It's a heartbreaking story of an unwanted pregnancy, which sees the desperate mother contemplate drowning the baby. Marr's marvellous melody fits the lyrics perfectly, and this is actually one of the best Smiths songs in their entire catalogue. It's a true masterpiece which was close to not being released at all.

'You've Got Everything Now' (Morrissey/Marr)
This version was recorded for the band's first David Jensen session for BBC Radio One in July 1983 and is a bit slower than the album version. Just like 'What Difference Does It Make?' and 'These Things Take Time', the drumming is more energetic and Paul Carrack's organ is missing.

'Accept Yourself' (Morrissey/Marr)
Originally released as a B-side to the second single, 'This Charming Man', this is the version recorded for the band's second David Jensen session in September 1983.

'Girl Afraid' (Morrissey/Marr)
(see 'Heaven Knows I'm Miserable Now' single)

'Back to the Old House' (Morrissey/Marr)
This song was originally released on the B-side to 'What Difference Does It Make?', but the version on this compilation was recorded for the Peel session in September 1983. This one is rather different from the recording made for the single, as it only features Morrissey, and Marr on his acoustic guitar, making it unique in The Smiths catalogue. Marr's fingerpicked melody is beautiful and melancholic (he reportedly wrote it with his then-girlfriend, now wife, Angie, in mind), which suits Morrissey's lyrics about not wanting to think about long lost love. The version released on the single features the full band, which doesn't really suit this song. It's a lot more beautiful with just the two songwriters doing what they do best.

'Reel Around the Fountain' (Morrissey/Marr)
Taken from the band's first Peel session in May 1983, this was a sneak peek at the forthcoming album, and compared to the John Porter produced version, this one lacks Paul Carrack's piano and organ. For some reason, it's also in a higher key and sounds a bit more urgent, especially Morrissey's vocals. This version was supposed to be The Smiths' second single but was replaced by 'This Charming Man' at the last second. Some test pressings were made, however, before the decision to go with another song, and those are now selling for ridiculous sums to collectors.

'Please, Please, Please Let Me Get What I Want' (Morrissey/Marr)
(see 'William, It Was Really Nothing' single)

The World Won't Listen (compilation, 1987)

Caryn Gough: layout
Jo Slee: art direction
Morrissey: sleeve
Playing time: 59:26
Label: Rough Trade (UK), Sire (US)
Release date: February 23rd 1987
Highest chart position: UK: 2

The success of the first compilation meant that it was just a matter of time before Rough Trade would put together a follow-up, and in early 1987 the band had released enough singles to fill two more sides of vinyl. The sixteen tracks were recorded from early 1985 up until early 1987, including seven singles and their B-sides, a new song ('You Just Haven't Earned It Yet, Baby'), and the fan favourite, 'There Is a Light That Never Goes Out' from 'The Queen Is Dead'. So no radio sessions this time around, but all the excellent singles made this a great package in its own right.

That The Smiths were a 'singles band' was quite obvious, but like The Beatles before them, they had enough great songs to put amazing tracks on the B-sides of the singles (they also made smashing albums, of course). They also decided to release a lot of non-album singles (like… well, The Beatles), making these compilations essential for the fans that hadn't bought the singles when they came out.

The cover art for this album contained a photo taken from a book with the snappy title 'Rock and Roll Times: The Style and Spirit of the Early Beatles and Their First Fans', which consisted of photos taken by German photographer Jürgen Vollmer. When the album art was reworked for the CD and cassette releases, the photo and artwork was cropped, which outraged Morrissey.

'Panic' (Morrissey/Marr)
(see 'Panic' single)

'Ask' (Morrissey/Marr)
(see 'Ask' single)

'London' (Morrissey/Marr)
(see 'Shoplifters of the World Unite' single)

'Bigmouth Strikes Again' (Morrissey/Marr)
(see under *The Queen Is Dead*)

'Shakespeare's Sister' (Morrissey/Marr)
(see 'Shakespeare's Sister' single)

'There Is a Light That Never Goes Out' (Morrissey/Marr)
(see under *The Queen Is Dead*)

'Shoplifters of the World Unite' (Morrissey/Marr)
(see 'Shoplifters of the World Unite' single)

'The Boy With the Thorn in His Side' (Morrissey/Marr)
(see under *The Queen Is Dead*)

'Asleep' (Morrissey/Marr)
Of all the morbid and suicidal Morrissey lyrics, this is probably the most explicit one, and one of the saddest songs any one could listen to. This is aided by the music, which is played like a lullaby on a piano (and the music box added to the end of the song). Like many people who had settled on going down the suicide path, the narrator in the song offers a gleam of positivity, as he thinks that there's a better world waiting for him 'on the other side'. The song was released as the B-side to 'The Boy With the Thorn in His Side' and was recorded on the same session as the other B-side, 'Rubber Ring'.

'Unloveable' (Morrissey/Marr)
Originally recorded for 'The Queen Is Dead', it was later replaced by 'Vicar in a Tutu' at the last second and was instead released on the B-side of 'Bigmouth Strikes Again'. The lyrics are yet another one of those 'self-pity' ones, which the title kind of gives away. The band never played the song live, which probably goes to show that it wasn't a favourite of theirs, and I guess the concert-goers weren't that disappointed either. That being said, this isn't a bad song at all; it's just a bit bleak compared to all the other brilliant songs surrounding it on this album.

'Half a Person' (Morrissey/Marr)
(see 'Shoplifters of the World Unite' single)

'Stretch Out and Wait' (Morrissey/Marr)
This song, released as the B-side to 'Shakespeare's Sister', is actually available in two slightly different versions. The one on this album has alternate lyrics during the first verse, and the one released on the single was later available on the 'Louder Than Bombs' compilation.

'That Joke Isn't Funny Anymore' (Morrissey/Marr)
This is basically the same version as on the 'Meat Is Murder' album, but the ending is fading out a bit earlier, as it's a radio edit.

'You Just Haven't Earned It Yet, Baby' (Morrissey/Marr)
This song was supposed to be the band's thirteenth single but was replaced by 'Shoplifters of the World Unite' at the last second. According to Marr, they

simply thought the latter was a better song, so it was thrown on to 'The World Won't Listen' as an exclusive, unreleased song instead. It was also reported that Morrissey didn't like all the overdubs that were made by John Porter (though another mix, with fewer overdubs, would soon be released on the *Louder Than Bombs* compilation). Ever since the song came out, it's been widely suggested that the lyrics were aimed at Rough Trade boss Geoff Travis, since the title was one of his favourite sayings, but Morrissey later stated that he never said it was aimed at Travis (even though he used the line again in the song 'Paint a Vulgar Picture' on *Strangeways, Here We Come*). The song was later recorded by Kirsty MacColl with Johnny Marr on guitar, in 1989.

'Rubber Ring' (Morrissey/Marr)

Released as a B-side to 'The Boy With the Thorn in His Side', the song kicks off with Rourke's funky bass and then evolves into Morrissey's ode to their most hardcore fans, asking them not to forget him as they grow older: 'But don't forget the songs that made you cry / And the songs that saved your life,' and also the line 'Do you love me like you used to?' The accompanying cello was reportedly played by Rourke (who also played cello on a couple of other Smiths songs), and the track ends with a couple of samples that Morrissey added. The first one to appear is from a 1953 recording of *The Importance of Being Ernest* by Oscar Wilde ('Is that clever?' and 'Everybody's clever nowadays'), and the second one, according to Simon Goddard in the book *Mozipedia,* was taken from a 7' single with a recorded translation of a seance that was held by Dr Konstantin Raudive. The message was received in Swedish ('Du sover') and German ('Du willst nicht glaube'), which translates into 'You are sleeping / You do not want to believe', the sample in the song being read by Nadia Fowler on the aforementioned 7' single. The Smiths never played the song live, but sometimes they added the intro from 'Rubber Ring' to 'What She Said' from *Meat Is Murder*, in concert (which can be heard on the live album *Rank*). On the original 12' release of 'The Boy With the Thorn in His Side', the two B-sides, 'Rubber Ring' and 'Asleep', appeared as a two-part song, where they slowly faded into each other, but they have since often been separated when included as part of compilations.

'Golden Lights' (Lynn Ripley)

This song wasn't on the original release of *The World Won't Listen* but has been added to all the subsequent reissues. More on the song when we discuss the 'Ask' single.

'Money Changes Everything' (Marr)

This 'Bigmouth Strikes Again' B-side was added to this compilation on the cassette versions and later CD reissues, and it's one of three instrumentals that The Smiths released (along with 'Oscillate Wildly' and 'The Draize Train'). The title is often seen as a stab at the band's label, Rough Trade, who they were fighting with a lot at the time. Morrissey's decision not to write any lyrics for the song didn't stop Marr taking it to his new friend Bryan Ferry, who used the song in a reworked form as the single 'The Right Stuff' in 1987.

Louder Than Bombs (compilation, 1987)

Caryn Gough: layout
Jo Slee: art direction
Morrissey: sleeve
Playing time: 72:44
Label: Rough Trade (UK), Sire (US)
Release date: March 30th 1987
Highest chart position: UK: 38, US: 62

As the previous compilation *Hatful of Hollow*, had been unavailable to the US fans (except as expensive import copies), their US label Sire decided to put together an extra compilation, intended for the US market only. It combined tracks from both *Hatful of Hollow* and *The World Won't Listen*, compiling most of the non-album songs from 1983 to 1987, and also the BBC session track, 'This Night Has Opened My Eyes'. As both 'This Charming Man' and 'How Soon Is Now?' had been released as bonus tracks on the US versions of the debut album and *Meat Is Murder,* they were omitted on this compilation.

The US only release of this album turned out to be an expensive affair for the completist UK fans, and rumours also spread that this was much better value for money, as it combined two compilations for the price of one. So, if you hadn't bought any of the two previous compilations, this was a way better deal! To stop expensive US copies being imported to the UK, Rough Trade finally gave in and released it in the UK as well, and it eventually peaked at #38 on the album charts.

The album actually gave some songs that were previously only available on singles their first UK album release. These included 'Sheila Take a Bow', 'Sweet and Tender Hooligan', 'Is It Really So Strange?', and the studio versions of 'These Things Take Time' and 'Back to the Old House'. The version of 'Stretch Out and Wait' is also different from the one on *The World Won't Listen*, with some alternate lyrics.

Nowadays, I suspect that most fans new to The Smiths will opt for this album instead of buying the other two collections.

The title, *Louder Than Bombs*, was taken from Elizabeth Smart's *By Grand Central Station I Sat Down and Wept*, and the cover star is author Shelagh Delaney, a photo taken from the newspaper *Saturday Evening Post*. Morrissey later said that this was his favourite Smiths sleeve.

'Is It Really So Strange?' (Morrissey/Marr)

One of the three songs that make up Morrissey's 'moving from the north to the south' trilogy (the other parts being 'London' and 'Half a Person'). It was originally recorded for the B-side of 'Ask' in June 1986, but the band wasn't happy with the recording, so the version of the song that was later released with 'Sheila Take a Bow' was taken from their last Peel session in late 1986 and it's also the version on this compilation. Of the three trilogy songs, this is by far the most humorous one, as Morrissey tells his tale of chasing his love interest all over the UK, during his travels killing both a nun and a horse, for some reason. Musically, it's yet another of the rockabilly influenced songs that the band recorded, although this is one of the slower ones.

'These Things Take Time' (Morrissey/Marr)

This song was included on the *Hatful of Hollow* compilation, but in its BBC session version, which is a bit rougher and rawer than the studio version that can be heard here. This version was on the B-side on the 12' version of 'What Difference Does It Make?'.

'Back to the Old House' (Morrissey/Marr)

As was the case with 'These Things Take Time', this song is also available in two different versions, where the BBC session version is the better one, with just Marr and Morrissey playing this lullaby-like tune together. The version available here was the one that appeared on the 'What Difference Does It Make?' single and features the entire band.

Rank (live album, 1988)

Craig Gannon: guitars
Caryn Gough: layout
Jo Slee: art direction
Morrissey: sleeve
Playing time: 55:56
Label: Rough Trade (UK), Sire (US)
Release date: September 5th 1988
Highest chart position: UK: 2, US: 77

When Morrissey released his first solo album, *Viva Hate*, in March 1988, the old Smiths fans started to yearn for their former idols, and they began to long for a reunion. As the band still had one more album to do for Rough Trade, they opted for the classic 'contractual obligation' solution by releasing a live album.

Rank was recorded at the National Ballroom in Kilburn, London on October 23rd 1986, during the band's tour for *The Queen Is Dead*, with Craig Gannon on second guitar. The original recording of the show is longer than the 56 minutes that ended up on the record (Morrissey chose which tracks should be on it), and some of the songs they left out from the show were 'There's A Light That Never Goes Out', 'I Want The One I Can't Have' and 'How Soon Is Now?'. According to author Johnny Rogan (who wrote *Morrissey and Marr – The Severed Alliance*), Morrissey's original title for the album was *The Smiths In Heat*, but the label didn't like it, so instead he went for *Rank*, allegedly taken from the British industralist J Arthur Rank (although that name is also a Cockney slang for 'wank').

Most of the songs on the album sounds more or less like their studio equivalent, but there are two medley exceptions. 'Rusholme Ruffians' (taken from *Meat Is Murder)* is played as a medley with 'His Latest Flame', a song made famous by Elvis Presley, and its melody sounds a lot like Marr's for 'Rusholme Ruffians'. Also, the band chose to play 'What She Said' (also taken from *Meat Is Murder*) as a medley with the B-side 'Rubber Ring'.

The cover star of the album is British actress Alexandra Bastedo, with a photo taken from the book *Birds Of Britain* (1967) by photographer John D Green.

On release, the album peaked at #2 in the UK, and when the album was released by Sire in the US, it didn't do as well, and peaked at #77 in the charts.

Part Two: Morrissey

Viva Hate (1988)

Personnel:
Morrissey: vocals, lyrics, sleeve art
Stephen Street: bass guitar, guitars, songwriter, producer
Vini Reilly: guitars, keyboards
Andrew Paresi: drums
Anton Corbijn: photography
Linder Sterling: photography
Eamon Macabe: photography
Caryn Gough: layout assistance
Jo Slee: art coordinator
Morrissey: sleeve
Recorded at Wool Hall Studios
Playing time: 42:16
Label: HMV (UK), Sire/Reprise (US)
Release date: March 14 1988
Highest chart position: UK: 1, US: 48

Released just six months after the last Smiths album, *Strangeways, Here We Come*, this was Morrissey's first solo outing, which found him working with former Smiths producer Stephen Street as his songwriting partner.

After The Smiths' painful split the year before, the pressure was now on the former frontman to deliver a solo record that was just as good as the albums that he recorded with his three former bandmates. And this debut would also be something of a test to see if he had what it took to be a solo artist, something that Morrissey himself never thought he would be. He always saw himself as the singer in a band, and not just any band – specifically The Smiths. When that band was no more, he didn't really know what to do. He even enlisted a replacement for Johnny Marr in The Smiths, guitarist Ivor Perry (former member of Easterhouse and The Cradle), but that didn't work out, so he had no choice but to go solo.

All the songs for the album were written by Morrissey and Street. Street sent the lyricist a tape of demos that he had recorded with The Smiths' B-sides in mind, but Morrissey came back to him and said that he wanted those songs to be part of his first solo album instead. Later on, the singer commented that he didn't really like the album as he thought that it was rushed. He was quite right about that. *Viva Hate* was both written and recorded quickly, with session musicians that were put together by Street (Morrissey asked both Rourke and Joyce to be part of his backing band, but they both said no). Street himself picked up the bass, and he asked Vini Reilly (from Factory label band Durutti Column) to play the guitar. As drummer, he picked Andrew Paresi (born Andrew McGibbon, now a comedian in the UK) – and voila – Morrissey had a new band!

Keeping with The Smiths tradition of having controversial lyrics, Morrissey also managed to get a few of those on his first solo album, with a touch of alleged racism and agitation. Such accusations of racism would go on to follow Morrissey throughout his solo career.

The album was a big success in the UK, where it went straight in at number one when it came out in March 1988. Since then, it has held its place among the classic Morrissey albums, and just like some of the later albums, its tracklist has been altered in later reissues, with different running orders and bonus tracks thrown in here and there. In the case of *Viva Hate*, the latest release (2012) omits the song 'The Ordinary Boys', which was replaced by 'Treat Me Like a Human Being' (a song that was recorded during the album sessions). The first major reissue of the album, in 1997 (to celebrate EMI's 100th anniversary), added eight bonus tracks taken from later single releases, and also changed the artwork of the album from the bluish photo on the original album to a new one with white background.

In Australia and New Zealand, the album was called *Education in Reverse*, as the local EMI branch didn't like the original title.

'Alsatian Cousin' (Morrissey/Street)

For fans of The Smiths hoping to get some more jangly pop tunes on Morrissey's first solo outing, this album opener must have come as something of a shock, with its screeching, distorted guitars and pounding drums. And where Marr always shied away from guitar solos, Morrissey's new guitar slinger Vini Reilly played like the song was one long solo. The song was written by Stephen Street, and his demo recording just featured a drum machine and the repetitive bass line (which he later admitted to borrowing from 'White Lines' by hip hop legends Grandmaster Flash & Melle Mel), with Reilly improvising his guitar lines on top. Reilly would later claim that he co-wrote the song with Street, wanting songwriter's royalties, but he never got them. The lyrics tell the story of a man who felt he had been cheated on, and interrogates the partner about the alleged fling: 'Were you and he lovers? / And would you say so if you were?'

'Little Man, What Now?' (Morrissey/Street)

Crossfading with 'Alsatian Cousins', the second song of the album has one of the more straightforward lyrics on *Viva Hate*, dealing with a youth actor who fades into obscurity when his acting career suddenly ends: he's 'too old to be a child star / too young to take leads'. Throughout the years, there have been many educated guesses about who the actor in question is, and in his book *Mozipedia*, Simon Goddard says that Malcolm McFee (who starred in the 60s and 70s British sitcom *Please Sir!)* was the most logical candidate. Morrissey himself had said that the character in the song was a real person, but that he didn't want to name names. Musically, the song continues in the more experimental style that was established in the previous track, with the steady rhythm being a loop of Andrew Paresi hitting a snare drum and a cymbal at the same time. Street also admitted that the flamenco style arrangement was borrowed from David Bowie's 'Andy Warhol'. Oh, and the title of the song was taken from a Hans Fallada novel of the same name.

'Everyday Is Like Sunday' (Morrissey/Street)

Arguably one of the most beloved and famous songs that Morrissey has ever been credited with, and the second single to be released off the album (peaking at #9), this one was featured on that first demo cassette that Street recorded for Morrissey just after The Smiths split up. It contains the classic Morrissey line 'Come come, nuclear bomb!', but even though he begs for Armageddon to come a bit earlier in the song, it is more likely a pop-drenched criticism of the Thatcher government and the way it messed up British society. The music video for the song was shot in Southend-on-Sea, but as Morrissey didn't show up for the filming, the director settled for Lucette Henderson, one of the girls that went on a bike ride with Morrissey in the video for 'I Started Something I Couldn't Finish', who spends a day in the life of Moz.

'Bengali in Platforms' (Morrissey/Street)

This is one of the first examples of Morrissey's alleged 'racist' lyrics, although Morrisey has himself said that he was 'not being deliberately provocative'. The lyrics deal with a person from Bengal who, on arrival in the UK, is trying his or her hardest to fit in, and adopts the lifestyle of the Western countries. One of the more controversial lines is probably 'life is hard enough when you belong here'. The song title actually dates back to mid-1987, when Morrissey still tried to keep going under The Smiths banner with Ivor Perry as Johnny Marr's replacement. Back then, the song was rather more reggae-rock than the gentle backing track that can be heard in the version on this album.

'Angel, Angel, Down We Go Together' (Morrissey/Street)

Another one of the songs on the Street demo cassette, this was Morrissey's favourite among the ideas that the producer sent to him for use as Smiths B-sides after Johnny Marr decided to leave the band, and the song was allegedly the one that made Morrissey put his old band to rest and instead embark on his solo career with Street. The backing track is provided by a string quartet (with music scored by John Metcalfe), and it's probably one of the shortest songs in the Morrissey catalogue, finishing after just a minute and a half. The lyricist has said that he wrote the song with Johnny Marr in mind, as a comment on his former bandmate's involvement in the music industry, and the lyrics seem to be about a suicidal person who's been treated really badly, by more or less everyone. The song was later rearranged by the rockabilly influenced backing band on the *Kill Uncle* tour in 1991, turning this harrowing string-based piece into a rock song.

'Late Night, Maudlin Street' (Morrissey/Street)

Closing the first side of the album, this near eight-minute-long journey through Morrissey's youth in Manchester is often considered one of the masterpieces of his solo career. There is no real Maudlin Street, but apart from that, the song is more or less autobiographical, and in the lyrics, Morrissey offers a powerful insight into his own insecurities when growing up ('but I cannot steal a pair of jeans off a clothesline for you / but you ... without clothes / Oh I could not keep a straight face / Me – without clothes? / Well, a nation turns its back and gags'). Musically, the song obviously doesn't want to steal Morrissey's thunder, as he delivers an almost uninterrupted vocal for the entire song – he specifically wanted Street to write 'a long, rambling track like Joni Mitchell'. Street later admitted that the drumbeat that goes on throughout the song was sampled from Prince's song 'Housequake'.

'Suedehead' (Morrissey/Marr)

Morrissey's first solo single, released on February 27th 1988 (peaking at #5 in the UK, which meant that it was more successful than any Smiths single), was also included on his first album, and along with 'Everyday Is Like Sunday', remains one of the most iconic solo Morrissey songs. The single actually came out just nine weeks after the final Smiths single, 'Last Night I Dreamt That Somebody Loved Me'. Fans of his former band were probably relieved when they heard the song, as it's not far from what Johnny Marr wrote for The Smiths, with its jangly guitars and great pop melody (it's actually one of few songs on the album that musically resembles The Smiths). There has been some speculation about the subject of the track, and some think that the lyrics were written with Marr in mind (as a kind of apology for the messy Smiths split – hence the chorus line 'I'm so sorry'), but while Morrissey has admitted that the song is about one specific person, he has never mentioned anyone in particular. During the recording of the song, Street and Reilly had an argument about the song's guitar break. Reilly didn't want to play it, as it was too easy, which meant that Street had to play it himself. The music video was directed by Morrissey's friend, Tim Broad, who also directed some of The Smiths' and most of Morrissey's videos until his death in 1993 and features the singer walking around in James Dean's hometown Fairmount, Indiana. The song was later remixed by Russell and Ron Mael of Sparks, originally for a compilation, and later on a Record Store Day 10' picture disc in 2012.

'Break Up the Family' (Morrissey/Marr)

Maybe 'the family' here was The Smiths? Well, that's probably what most fans thought when they heard the song, which was written and recorded just a short while after the band's demise. But in fact the song is set far earlier than that, in 1972. Morrissey talked about the lyrics at the time of the album's release and said that 'the family' in this case was a group of friends that he used to spend a lot of time with in his youth. For them to be able to move on in life, they had to split up and go their separate ways. Musically, the arrangement is quite simple, with Paresi's steady beat being one of the most audible instruments in the mix.

'The Ordinary Boys' (Morrissey/Marr)

For reasons probably only known to Morrissey himself, he chose to omit this track for the 2012 reissue and instead replaced it with 'Treat Me Like a Human Being', which makes this song unavailable to anyone who hasn't got the previous releases. And sure, this may not be the highlight of the album, but at least it's better than its replacement. The lyrics are another of Mozzer's celebrations of outsiders – the ones who dare to be different. Street wrote the song as a piano ballad, with Morrissey adding some nice falsettos here and there. Street isn't very fond of the song, and thinks that it's the weakest song of the album alongside 'Margaret on the Guillotine'.

'I Don't Mind if You Forget Me' (Morrissey/Street)

Throughout The Smiths short history, Morrissey often returned to the scary thought of being forgotten ('Little Man, What Now?' on this album is also on the same subject), but here he's saying the opposite, or that's what you're supposed to think, anyway. Most fans are convinced that the song is another one of Morrissey's 'Smiths break-up songs', and that the lines 'Rejection is one thing / But rejection from a fool is cruel' were aimed at Johnny Marr. Well, Morrissey himself has never commented on the song, but the interpretation is not that far-fetched. Street wrote the music as a mix between Motown and Buzzcocks; it's hardly a fan favourite.

'Dial-a-Cliche' (Morrissey/Street)

Keeping with the tradition of less-liked songs, this is another one. 'Dial-a-Cliche' was one of the first songs to be written and recorded for the album, and neither Paresi or Reilly liked it, with the former calling it 'too wimpy' – and he does have a point – even though I wouldn't call it TOO wimpy myself. The lyrics once again throw us back to Morrissey's youth and deal with the pressure from society to adapt to the male stereotypes ('yet still you say / 'Do as I do and scrap your fey ways' / Dial-a-cliche / 'Grow up, be a man, and close your mealy-mouth!' / Dial-a-cliche / 'The safe way is the only way, there's always time to change, son!' / Yes, well, I've changed, but I'm in pain!').

'Margaret on the Guillotine' (Morrissey/Street)

The album closer is also one of the most controversial songs on the album, with its not-so-subtle attack on prime minister Margaret Thatcher that made the Special Branch, which deals with aspects of national security in the UK, bring in Morrissey for questioning. The song hasn't made it to the Moz history books as one of his best ones, but I believe that it does deserve its place in them, because of the explicitly political lyrics. The song title was actually the working title of 'The Queen Is Dead', one of the few other political lyrics by Morrissey.

Street wasn't a fan of this one either, as he felt that the lyrics were a bit too full on, and he probably had a softer intention when he wrote the rather nice melody. The song ends with Reilly's flamenco influenced acoustic guitar solo, which is brutally cut short with the sound of a guillotine chop. A dramatic close to a great first album!

'Hairdresser on Fire' (Morrissey/Street)

Well, even though the UK album closed with 'Margaret on the Guillotine', we still have a couple of songs to deal with here. On the US release of *Viva Hate*, the label chose to include this song, which was originally released on the 'Suedehead' 12' single. EMI really wanted Morrissey to include the song on the album in the UK as well, but he didn't think it was a good idea at the time (it would later be included on the forthcoming *Bona Drag* compilation, though). When it comes to the lyrics to this great little pop tune, Morrissey once said that it was 'a very simple song about trying to get hold of a hairdresser', which would probably make it one of his most straightforward lyrics ever ('Oh, hairdresser on fire / All around Sloane Square / And you're far too busy to see me'). The song was also released as a one-sided single that was included with the Japanese version of the album.

'Treat Me Like a Human Being' (Morrissey/Street)

As mentioned earlier, Morrissey decided to omit that song when the album was re-released in 2012 and opted for this one instead. It was recorded during the *Viva Hate* sessions but never made it to the album, as both Morrissey and Street felt that the other songs were better. The lyrics find the singer begging to be... well, treated like a human being ('Treat me like a human being / I'd like to know how this feels') instead asking for 'three words'. It's hard not to interpret the lyrics as a comment on The Smiths split (which happened just a few months before this song was written), the title being an obvious plea to Johnny Marr. Musically, the only surprising element is the sitar-like guitar – apart from that, there is not a lot to write home about here.

Contemporary Tracks

'I Know Very Well How I Got My Name' (Morrissey/Street)

This was the B-side to Morrissey's first solo single, 'Suedehead', in 1988, and it features just Morrissey and guitarist Vini Reilly, plus a delicate string arrangement. The lyrics feature some snapshots from Moz's youth, including the tale of him trying to dye his hair gold in 1972 to be like Ziggy Stardust (it eventually turned purple, and he was sent home from school, he later admitted in an interview). In 1989, an alternative version of the song surfaced, as Reilly released a demo called 'I Know Very Well How I Got My Note Wrong' on a freebie that came with his band Durutti Column's album, *Vini Reilly*. The recording ends with Reilly playing a false note, which makes both Morrissey and Reilly crack up.

'Oh Well, I'll Never Learn' (Morrissey/Street)

Another B-side to 'Suedehead', this is also a sparse recording, with just Morrissey, Reilly (probably) and a tambourine. According to Street, he wrote a song that would resemble an early Velvet Underground ballad, he succeeds in that. Morrissey sings about him not being able to learn from the mistakes he's made in life, but in the end, he sings 'Why should I mind? Why should I care?', so maybe he… well… doesn't mind.

Contemporary Singles

The Last of the Famous International Playboys (single, 1989)

Personnel:
Morrissey: vocals, sleeve design
Craig Gannon: guitars
Neil Taylor: guitars
Andy Rourke: bass guitar
Stephen Street: keyboards, production
Mike Joyce: drums

'The Last of the Famous International Playboys' (Morrissey/Street)

Morrissey's third, and first non-album, single was released on January 30th 1989 and climbed to #6 on the UK singles chart. The song was written with Street, who later said that he wanted to write a punky song, like The Fall, with simple chords and a thumping backing track, and he succeeded. Before recording the song, Morrissey kicked out Vini Reilly and Andrew Paresi, who played on the *Viva Hate* album, and to replace them, he brought in his old bandmates Rourke, Joyce, and Gannon, plus Neil Taylor as an extra guitarist. In the lyrics, Morrissey recalled the days of the infamous Kray Twins (Ronnie and Reggie), two notorious criminals that haunted London in the 60s, expanding on Morrissey's love of 50s and 60s gangster culture (he would later send a wreath to Reggie's funeral in 2000). The single sleeve sports a photo of a young Morrissey sitting in a tree.

'Lucky Lisp' (Morrissey/Street)

In 1956, Ruth Brown recorded a song by songwriters extraordinaire Jerry Lieber and Mike Stoller called 'Lucky Lips'. Seven years later, Cliff Richard had a huge international hit with his version, and in 1989 Morrissey decided that it was a great idea to record a song with the pun title 'Lucky Lisp'. The latter was featured on the B-side of 'The Last of the Famous International Playboys' single and was co-written with Street. It's probably one of the first examples of Morrissey using synthesizers in his music (he would take that much further a few decades later), but despite the bad pun, it's actually quite a good pop song, with former Smiths member Gannon getting the chance to shine with some jangly guitars.

'Michael's Bones' (Morrissey/Street)

Allegedly, the 'Michael' mentioned in this song is a mass murderer called Michael Ryan, who killed sixteen people in the town of Hungerford back in August 1987, but Morrissey has never confirmed this. A rather spooky coincidence is that the release of The Smiths single 'Stop Me if You Think You've Heard This One Before' was cancelled in the autumn of 1987 because of that same massacre, as Morrissey sings of planning a mass murder in the lyrics. Street's tune is a slow, melancholic affair, and it was the first song the band recorded while staying at The Wool Hall to record the 'Interesting Drug' single (which was to be the next Morrissey release, in April 1989).

Interesting Drug (single, 1989)

Personnel:
Morrissey: vocals, sleeve design
Craig Gannon: guitars
Neil Taylor: guitars
Andy Rourke: bass guitar
Stephen Street: keyboards, production
Mike Joyce: drums
Kirsty MacColl: backing vocals

'Interesting Drug' (Morrissey/Street)

This was Morrissey's fourth solo single, originally released on April 17 1989, eventually peaking at #9 in the UK (his last single to reach the top 10 for five years). Three of his former Smiths colleagues (Rourke, Joyce and Gannon) played on this song, and it was produced by Stephen Street, who also plays keyboards (Moz's friend Kirsty MacColl also stopped by the studio to sing some lovely backing vocals). Joyce's jittery drum beat provides the backing to Gannon and Neil Taylor's jangly guitars on this 'Madchester' (eg. bands like The Stone Roses and Happy Mondays) influenced track. Morrissey sings about the poor working class, where people use drugs to escape their bleak reality, putting the blame on the Thatcher government which created such social differences. At the time, Moz was criticised for romanticising drug use, as he sings that they 'really helped you', and he later said that those lines were maybe a bit 'too direct'. The music video for the song was directed by Tim Broad, and in it you can see the words 'bad people on the right' written on a wall. I wonder if Morrissey still agrees with that today.

'Such a Little Thing Makes Such a Big Difference' (Morrissey/Street)

This song was written by Street as a homage to the US duo Sparks, as requested by Morrissey, who was a big fan of Sparks, and they would later record a song called 'Lighten Up, Morrissey', about dating a girl who's obsessed with the singer. Street later said that the song was written in the studio at The Wool

Hall in Bath while recording 'The Last of the Famous International Playboys' and 'Interesting Drug'. When played live, it was often played as a medley with either the very early Suede song 'My Insatiable One' or Morrissey's own 'I Know It's Gonna Happen Someday' (from *Your Arsenal*). The lyrics are a comment on love (and hate) with Moz commenting that 'some people keep their brain between their legs'.

'Sweet and Tender Hooligan – Live' (Morrissey/Marr)

The Smiths never played this surprisingly punky song live during their lifetime, but Morrissey decided to play it as an encore, when he played his first-ever solo gig in Wolverhampton in December 1988, and this recording is from that show, with Rourke and Joyce in the band. More on the song itself can be found on The Smiths' 'Sheila Take a Bow' single (1987).

Ouija Board, Ouija Board (single, 1989)

Personnel:
Morrissey: vocals, sleeve design
Kevin Armstrong: guitars
Matthew Seligman: bass guitar
Steve Hopkins: piano
Andrew Paresi: drums
Kirsty MacColl: backing vocals

'Ouija Board, Ouija Board' (Morrissey/Street)

So, we have come to this – the second turning point in Morrissey's solo career, and this one was not of the good kind. Released on November 13th 1989, this was Morrissey's fifth single, and it was the first one not to reach the top 10 on the singles chart (it peaked at #18). Not only was it a commercial disappointment, but it was also butchered by the music critics, sending Moz into a depression that made him abort the ongoing recording sessions for his second album. The song was written with Street, but financial disagreements with Moz made him refuse to produce it, and the singer instead enlisted Langer and Winstanley as a plan B to save the project. He also replaced some of the musicians, with Kevin Armstrong stepping in as guitarist, Matthew Seligman (former member of The Soft Boys and an early lineup of The Thompson Twins) on bass, while Kirsty MacColl once again sang some beautiful backing vocals. In the lyrics, Moz tries to get in touch with an old dead friend with the help of an Ouija board, but she tells him, via the glass, to 'push off'. According to Armstrong, Morrissey held a real Ouija board session, as the studio was rumoured to be haunted, and the guitarist claimed that things did happen for real on the board.

'Yes, I Am Blind' (Morrissey/Rourke)

This song was co-written with Andy Rourke, though he doesn't play on the recording. Rourke had recorded a demo version for Morrissey earlier in 1989, and it was later copied by Armstrong and Matthew Seligman when they came to record the song during the 'Ouija Board' sessions. This is yet another example of the great songs that Morrissey stuck away on B-sides: it would have been a great addition to the *Viva Hate* album if it had been recorded during those sessions.

'East West' (Graham Gouldman)

This song was originally recorded by 60s pop stars Herman's Hermits (also from Manchester), and released as a single in 1966, although it didn't manage to climb any higher than #33 in the UK. It was written by master songwriter Graham Gouldman (co-founder of 10cc and Wax, and also a songwriter for The Yardbirds and Herman's Hermits, among others). As Herman's Hermits version was released just before Christmas, the last verse of the song had something of a holiday theme, with references to parents sitting around the fire in festive attire, which would have been a bit out of place for Morrissey's version, so he decided to make a few changes in that verse to make it more suitable (he also changed a few bits more here and there). The main theme of the song, being out travelling the world but longing to go home, is still there.

November Spawned a Monster (single, 1990)

Personnel:
Morrissey: vocals
Kevin Armstrong: guitars
Andy Rourke: bass guitar
Andrew Paresi: drums
Mary Margaret O'Hara: backing vocals

'November Spawned a Monster' (Morrissey/Langer)

This was Morrissey's sixth solo single, released on April 23 1990, peaking at #12 in the UK. A few years later, Morrissey described this as a turning point in his career, and the first time that he didn't miss Marr as a songwriting partner, realising that he was better off without him. And it's not hard to understand why he was happy with this one. Written with producer Clive Langer, it was played by Rourke, Paresi and Armstrong, with Canadian singer Mary Margaret O'Hara singing the harrowing backing vocals (meant to represent the spawning of the monster). In the lyrics, Moz tried to imagine the frustrations of a wheelchair-bound girl (the 'monster'), and the prejudices (and also sympathy) that she encounters in life. The music video was once again directed by Tim Broad, showing Morrissey seemingly humping various rock formations in Death Valley, prompting the MTV cartoon teens Beavis & Butthead to mock it in one of the show's episodes. The song is one of Moz's personal favourites, and he still played it live as late as 2018.

'He Knows I'd Love To See Him' (Morrissey/Armstrong)

Co-written with guitarist Armstrong, this was a rare acoustic recording at this point in Morrissey's solo career, not so far away from the future 'Driving Your

Girlfriend Home' (from his next album, *Kill Uncle*). The double bass was played by the legendary Danny Thompson (but he never received any credit for it), who was a member of Pentangle in the 60s and 70s and also played on Nick Drake's debut album. There are also some nice backing vocals, sung by Mary Margaret O'Hara. In the lyrics, Morrissey refers to Manchester as 'the arse of the world', which really comes as no surprise considering previous lyrics concerning his hometown.

'The Girl Least Likely To' (Morrissey/Rourke)

Quite surprisingly, this song with constantly changing chords was co-written by former Smiths colleague Andy Rourke; he also wrote 'Yes I Am Blind' on the previous single, but this time he got to play on his own song! The band recorded it for the aborted *Bona Drag* album (the title was then used for the compilation that came out in 1990), but instead, it ended up on this B-side. In later interviews, Morrissey admitted that the real-life 'girl' in the lyrics actually guessed that she was the one in the song, and got quite mad at him, which might not be that surprising, as Moz sings about a girl who has her heart set on success, but he already knows that she will fail.

Bona Drag (compilation, 1990)

Personnel:
Morrissey: vocals, sleeve design
Kevin Armstrong: guitars
Vini Reilly: guitars, piano
Craig Gannon: guitars
Neil Taylor: guitars
Andy Rourke: bass guitar
Matthew Seligman: bass guitar
Stephen Street: bass guitar, keyboards
Andrew Paresi: drums
Mike Joyce: drums
Jo Slee: art coordinator
Juergen Teller: photography
Produced by Clive Langer, Alan Winstanley and Stephen Street
Playing time: 49 min 45 sec
Label: HMV (UK), Sire/Reprise (US), Major Minor (reissue 2010)
Release date: October 15 1990
Highest chart position: UK: 9, US: 59

After the success with *Viva Hate*, the pressure was on once again, this time to record an equally successful second solo album both critically and commercially. What looked like a bad start would soon turn around, and then turn around once again, within just a few months.

First of all, Mike Joyce and Craig Gannon both left Morrissey's band due to financial disagreements from their time in The Smiths (the Joyce case would haunt Morrissey for years to come), and initially, Andy Rourke left as well, but he eventually settled his case out of court and was then welcomed back to the Moz camp again. However, he still needed a new drummer and guitarist, so he asked Andrew Paresi, who played the drums on *Viva Hate* (and was replaced by Joyce for the big debut solo gig in Wolverhampton on December 22 1988), to come back, and he also recruited guitarist Kevin Armstrong, who had previously worked with Paresi on Sandie Shaw's album *Hello Angel* in 1988, where she recorded two songs by Morrissey ('Hand in Glove' and 'Please Help The Cause Against Loneliness', written with Stephen Street). He had also been suggested by Rough Trade to replace Johnny Marr in The Smiths when the latter left, but nothing happened at that point. And the bad news didn't stop there. Producer Stephen Street also decided to move on to other things, so Morrissey had to find a new producer as well, eventually choosing the classic duo Clive Langer and Alan Winstanley.

With his new crew in place, things finally started to look bright again for Morrissey, and they all convened at the Hook End Manor studio to record the second solo album, which had the working title *Bona Drag* (a title taken from the slang language Palare, popularised on the 60s BBC radio series *Round the Horne*. It means 'good clothes'). But then, during the recording sessions, Morrissey released the single 'Ouija Board, Ouija Board'. It was butchered by the music critics and was the first Morrissey solo single not to crack the top 20. Armstrong later said that this was a huge blow to Moz and that he became depressed for a period of time. That also meant that the sessions were abandoned, and the album was shelved.

But Morrissey still wanted to keep up the momentum, so instead of releasing an album containing new music, the label opted for a compilation that collected all the seven singles he had released so far, plus most of the B-sides. It was originally meant for the US and international market, where the singles were harder to come by, but in the end, it was released in the UK as well, to great acclaim, as the album showed what great singles Moz had released since his Smiths days. Just like his former band, he had kept up the tradition of releasing non-album singles, with mostly great B-sides.

The cover photo for the album was taken from the music video for 'November Spawned a Monster', but the screenshot was altered a bit, as Moz suddenly wore a red shirt and a white undershirt on the sleeve. When the album was re-released for its 20th anniversary in 2010, the cover photo was altered yet again, and this time the shirt was black again, and the blue background was now white-beige. Along with the changes in the graphics, six unreleased studio outtakes were added.

The compilation meant that Morrissey could focus on his proper second album, and when *Bona Drag* was released in October 1990, he was already recording *Kill Uncle* with some more new band members.

'Piccadilly Palare' (Morrissey/Armstrong)

Released as a single on the same day as the album, October 8, 1990, it peaked at #13, despite not getting any promotion worth mentioning – there was no video made, for example. Morrissey himself wasn't very fond of the song, even back then, and in his autobiography, he maintained this view. And you can't blame him, really. Musically, it resembles Madness, the band that producers Langer and Winstanley had worked with earlier in the 80s, with its stomping piano-based rhythm (for an added Madness touch, their lead singer Graham 'Suggs' McPherson joins in on backing vocals) – and lyrically, it's a visit to the male prostitution hoods around Piccadilly, which makes this one of many Moz songs about the gay community. The bass on the song is played by Andy Rourke, and this is the last recording on which Morrissey played with any of his former bandmates.

'Interesting Drug' (Morrissey/Street)

(see 'Interesting Drug' single)

'November Spawned a Monster' (Morrissey/Langer)

(see 'November Spawned a Monster' single)

'Will Never Marry' (Morrissey/Street)
Originally released as the B-side to 'Everyday Is Like Sunday' in 1988, this epic ballad was written with Stephen Street, and here Morrissey shares his rather bleak views on marriage. He had previously said in interviews that he never had known of a happy marriage (his own parents divorced when he was seventeen), and here he stated that he couldn't see himself ever marrying someone and as far as we know, he never has. The majestic string arrangement was written by John Metcalfe (of Durutti Column), and the woman shouting 'Steven!' at the end of the song is Stephen Street's wife Sarah, who happened to visit the studio with their son the day they recorded this song. When played live, the piano arrangement was scrapped in favour of guitars to suit the live band better. The version featured on *Bona Drag* was edited from the B-side and omits the last section of the song.

'Such a Little Thing Makes Such a Big Difference' (Morrissey/Street)
(see 'Interesting Drug' single)

'The Last of the Famous International Playboys' (Morrissey/Street)
(see 'The Last of the Famous International Playboys' single)

'Ouija Board, Ouija Board' (Morrissey/Street)
(see 'Ouija Board, Ouija Board' single)

'Hairdresser on Fire' (Morrissey/Street)
(see *Viva Hate*)

'Everyday Is Like Sunday' (Morrissey/Street)
(see *Viva Hate*)

'He Knows I'd Love To See Him' (Morrissey/Armstrong)
(see 'November Spawned a Monster' single)

'Yes, I Am Blind' (Morrissey/Rourke)
(see 'Ouija Board, Ouija Board' single)

'Lucky Lisp' (Morrissey/Street)
(see 'The Last of the Famous International Playboys' single)

'Suedehead' (Morrissey/Street)
(see *Viva Hate*)

'Disappointed' (Morrissey/Street)
Originally released as a B-side to 'Everyday Is Like Sunday' in 1988, this song

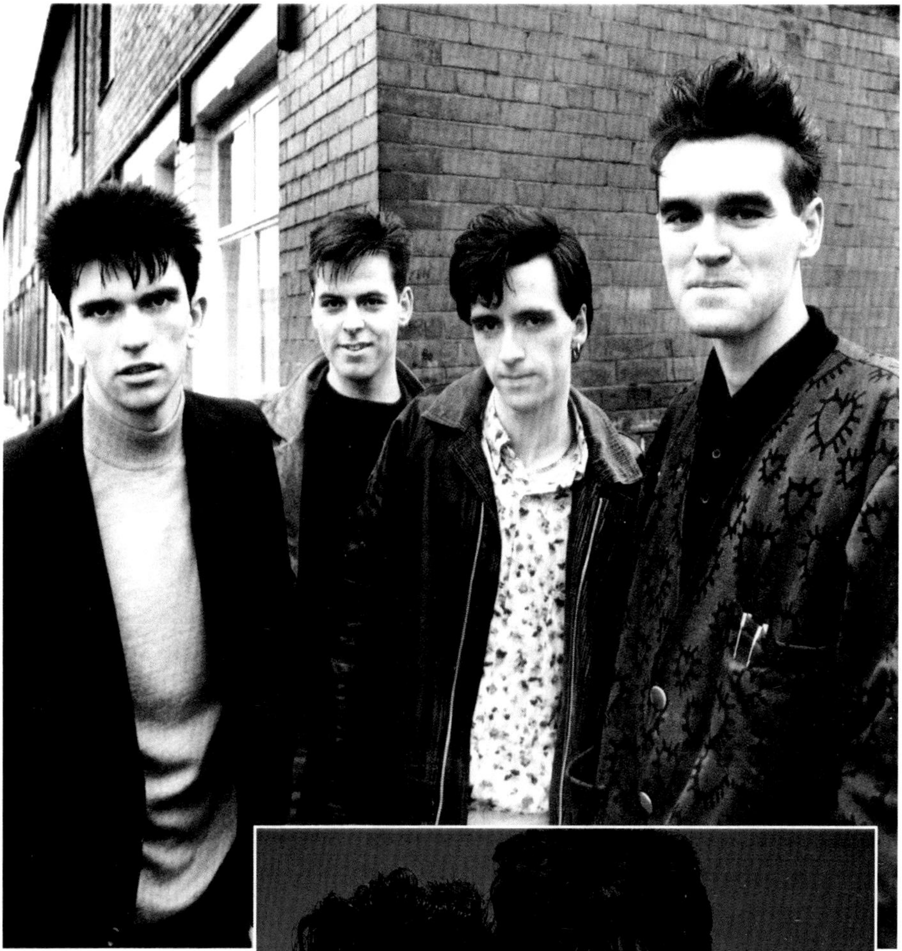

Above: The Smiths posing at Coronation Street in December 1985. (*Stephen Wright*)

Above: Morrissey and Marr before falling out, in 1987. (*Eugene Adebari*)

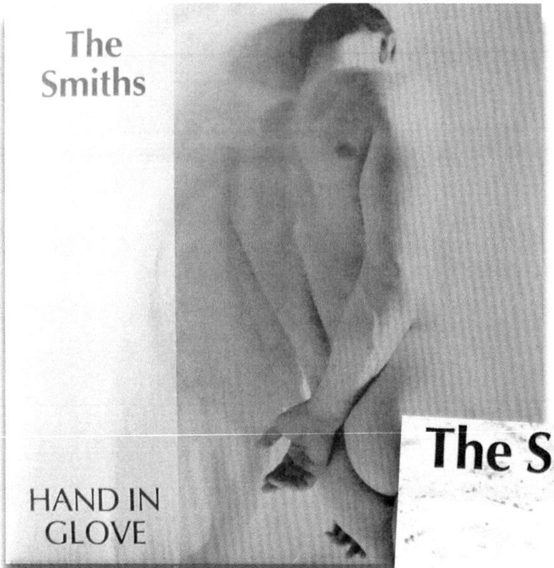

Left: The debut single, released on Rough Trade in May 1983. Cover star unknown. (*Rough Trade/Warner*)

Right: 'This Charming Man', their first hit single, released in October 1983. Cover star: Jean Marais. (*Rough Trade/Warner*)

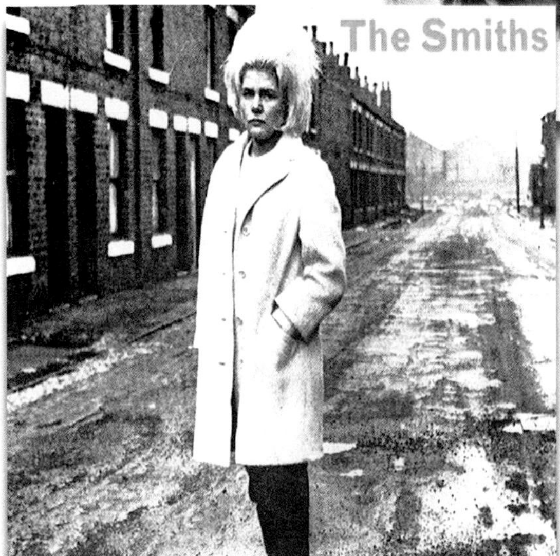

Left: 'Heaven Knows I'm Miserable Now', released in May 1984. Cover star: Viv Nicholson. (*Rough Trade/Warner*)

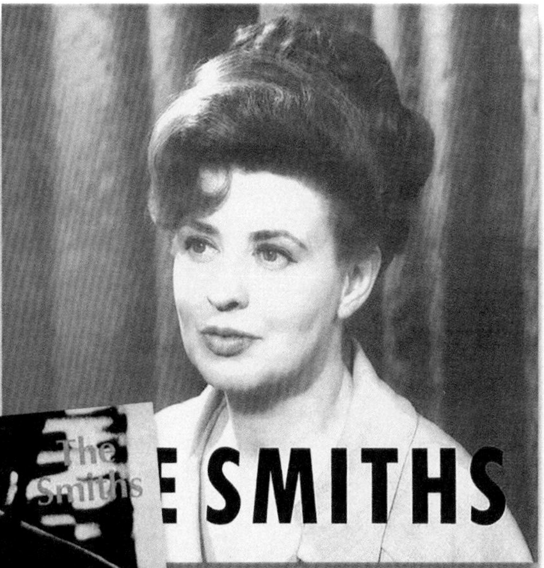

Right: 'Shakespeare's Sister', released in March 1985. Cover star: Pat Phoenix. (*Rough Trade/Warner*)

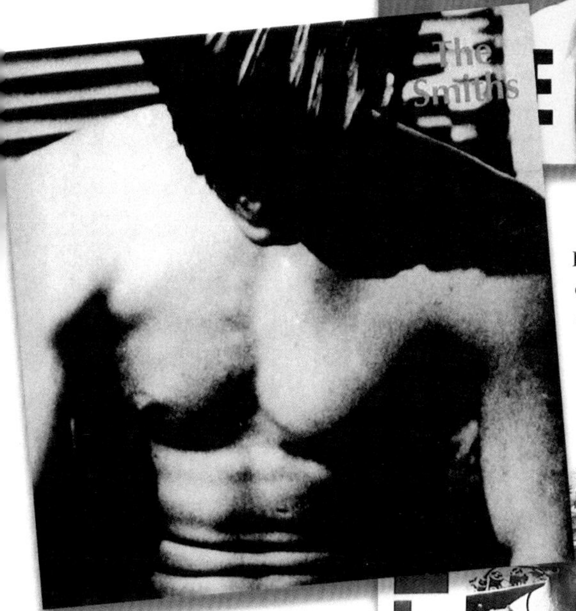

Left: The self-titled debut album, released in February 1984. Cover star: Joe Dallesandro. (*Rough Trade/Warner*)

Right: The second album, *Meat Is Murder*, released in February 1985. Cover star: Cpl Michael Wynn. (*Rough Trade/Warner*)

Left: That iconic third album, released in June 1986. Cover star: Alain Delon. (*Rough Trade/ Warner*)

Right: The last studio album, released in September 1987, after the band had disbanded. Cover star: Richard Davalos. (*Rough Trade/Warner*)

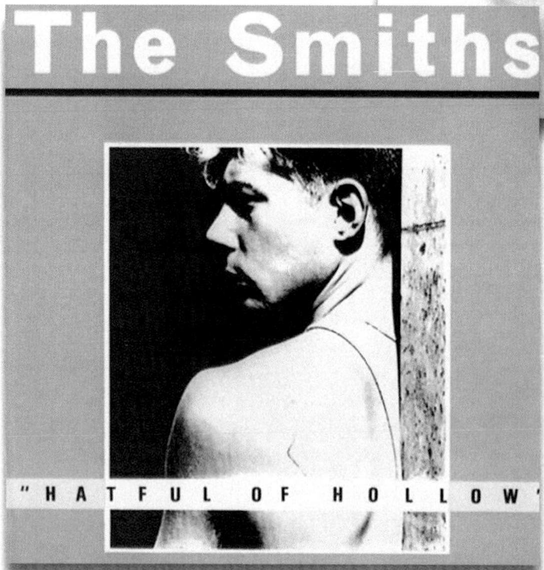

Left: The first compilation, containing singles, B-sides and sessions, released in November 1984. Cover star: Fabrice Colette. (*Rough Trade/Warner*)

Right: The second compilation of singles and B-sides, released in February 1987. Cover stars: unknown. (*Rough Trade/Warner*)

Left: Initially released for the US market, this combination of *Hatful Of Hollow* and *The World Won't Listen* was released in March 1987. Cover star: Shelagh Delaney. *(Rough Trade/Warner)*

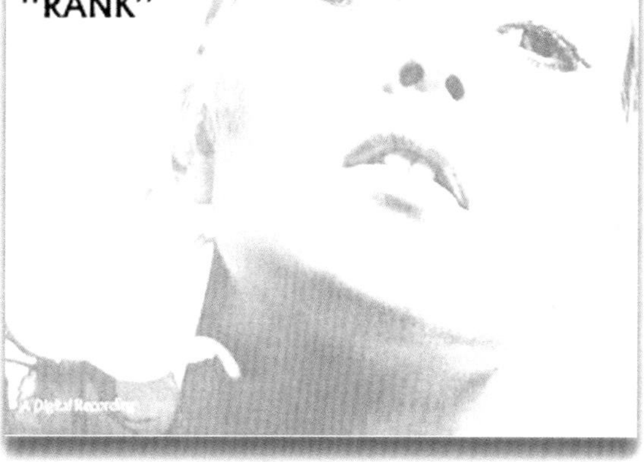

Right: The only live album released by The Smiths, recorded during the *Queen Is Dead* tour in 1986 and released in September 1988. Cover star: Alexandra Bastedo. (*Rough Trade/Warner*)

Left: Johnny Marr performing 'What Difference Does It Make?' on BBC's *Top of the Pops* in January 1984. (*BBC*)

Right: Mike Joyce during the same performance. (*BBC*)

Left: Finally, Andy Rourke during the same song. (*BBC*)

Right: Morrissey performing 'Heaven Knows I'm Miserable Now' on BBC's *Top of the Pops* again in June 1984. (*BBC*)

Left: Johnny Marr performing the same song on 'Top Of The Pops' in June 1984. (*BBC*)

Right: Andy Rourke, Morrissey and Johnny Marr during the same show. (*BBC*)

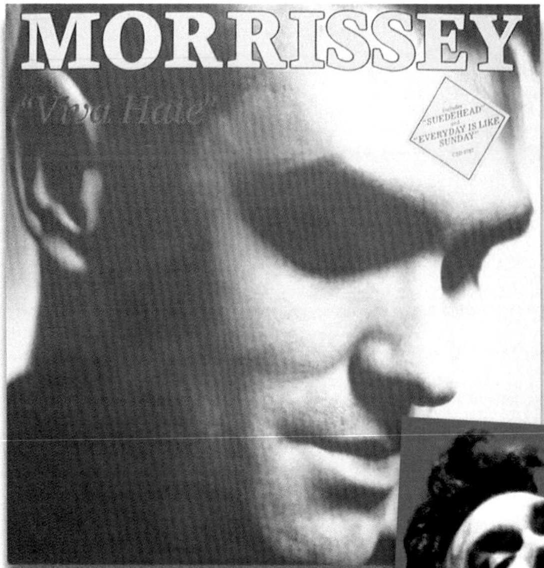

Left: The original sleeve design of Morrissey's first solo album, released in March 1988. It was redesigned in 1997 and 2012. (*Parlophone/Warner*)

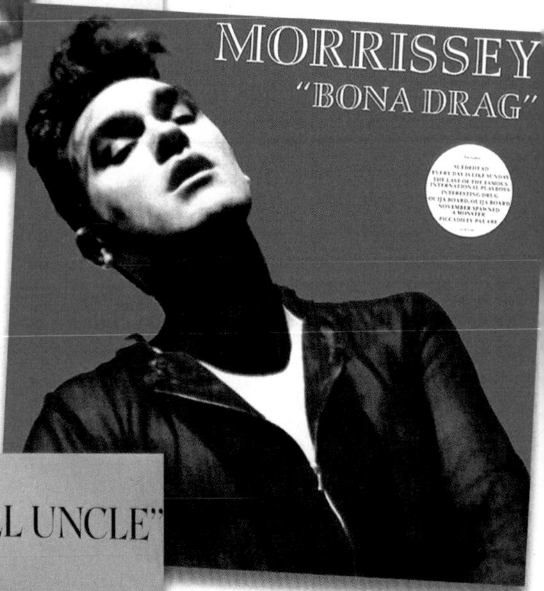

Right: Original sleeve design for Moz's first solo compilation, with singles and B-sides, released in October 1990. It was slightly redesigned in 2010. (*Parlophone/Warner*)

Left: Original sleeve design for the second studio album, released in March 1991. It was redesigned with a different photo of Moz in 2013. (*HMV/Warner*)

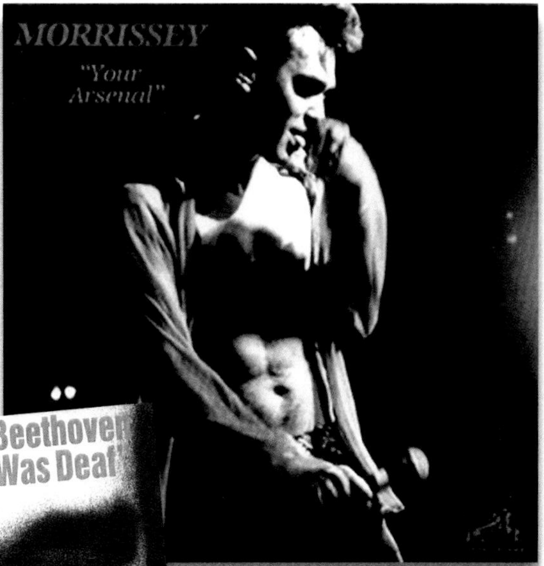

Right: The third solo album, released in July 1992, the first one with new songwriter Alain Whyte. (*HMV/Warner*)

Left: Morrissey's first live album, recorded in Paris and London in December 1992. Released in May 1993. (*HMV/Parlophone*)

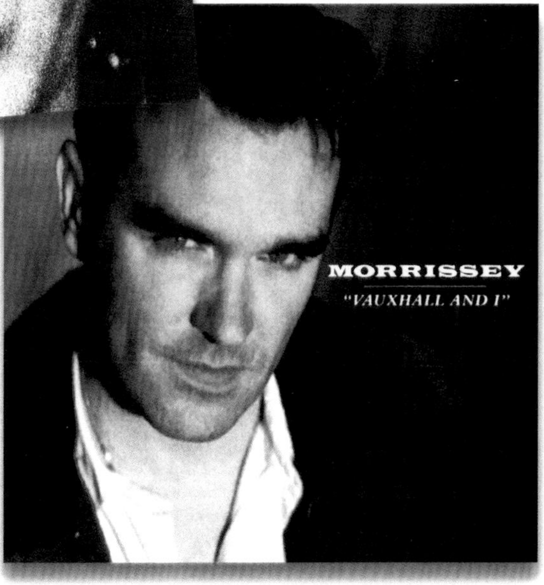

Right: *Vauxhall and I*. Morrissey's masterpiece, according to many fans. Released as his fourth solo album in March 1994. (*Parlophone/Warner*)

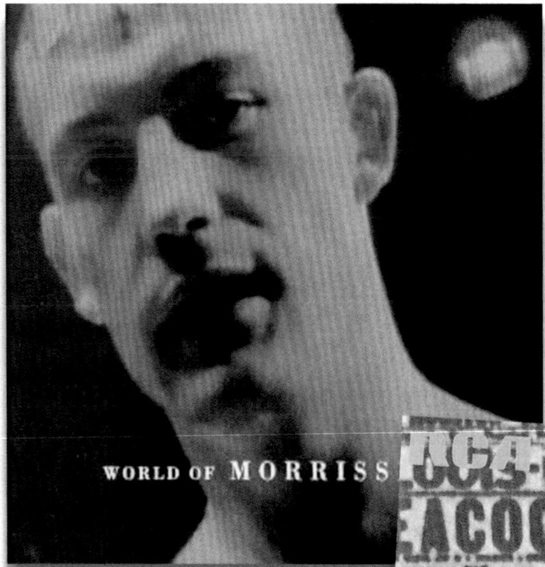

Left: Morrissey's second solo compilation, consisting of singles and live tracks, released in February 1995. Cover star: Cornelius Carr. (*Parlophone/Warner*)

Right: The original sleeve design for Morrissey's fifth studio album, released in August 1995. Cover star: Kenny Lane. It was redesigned in 2009 with Moz on the cover. (*RCA/BMG*)

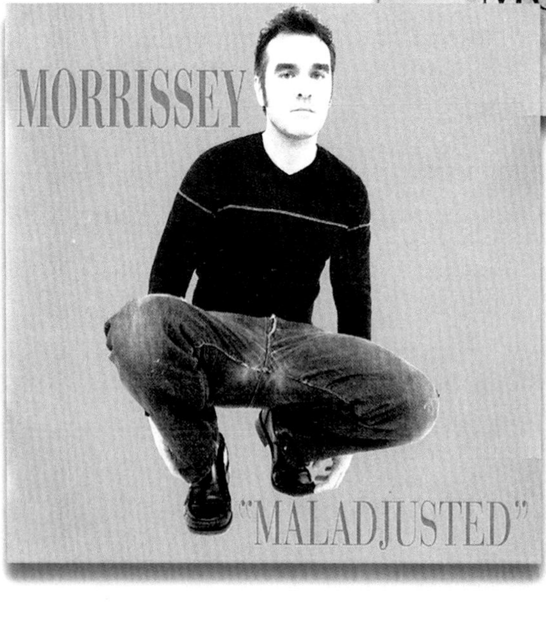

Left: The original sleeve design for the sixth studio album, released in August 1997. It was redesigned with a new photo of Moz in 2009. (*Mercury/Universal*)

Right: Morrissey's seventh solo album, which marked a comeback after almost seven years. Released in May 2004. (*Sanctuary/BMG*)

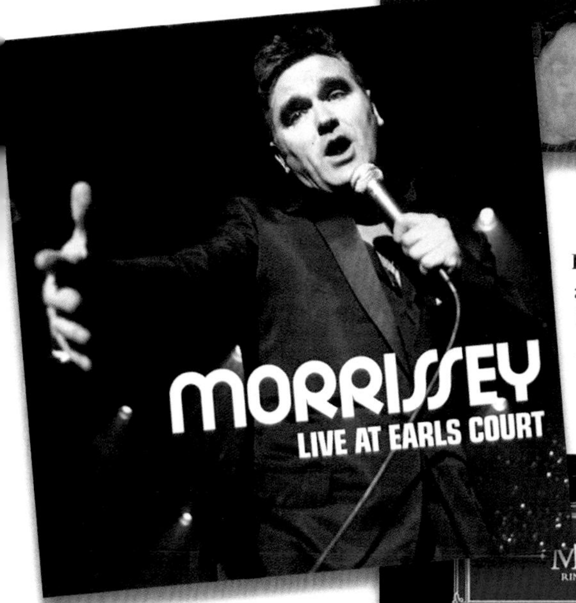

Left: Morrissey's second live album, recorded in London in December 2004. Released in April 2005. (*Sanctuary/BMG*)

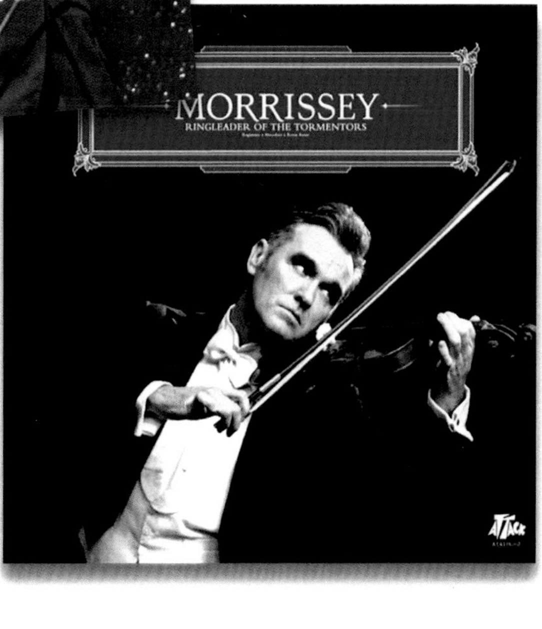

Right: The eighth studio album, recorded in Italy with producer Tony Visconti and released in April 2006. (*Sanctuary/BMG*)

Left: Morrissey performing in Las Vegas in August 2021.

Right: Morrissey performing in Manchester on his birthday on 22 May in 2004. Taken from the DVD *Who Puts the M In Manchester*. (*Sanctuary/BMG*)

Left: Still from the 'Dagenham Dave' music video, released in August 1995. (*RCA/BMG*)

Right: Morrissey performing for a BBC6 Music show in London in October 2017. (*BBC*)

Left: Performing at the same show in London in October 2017. (*BBC*)

Right: Matthew Ira Walker performing with Morrissey at the same show. (BBC)

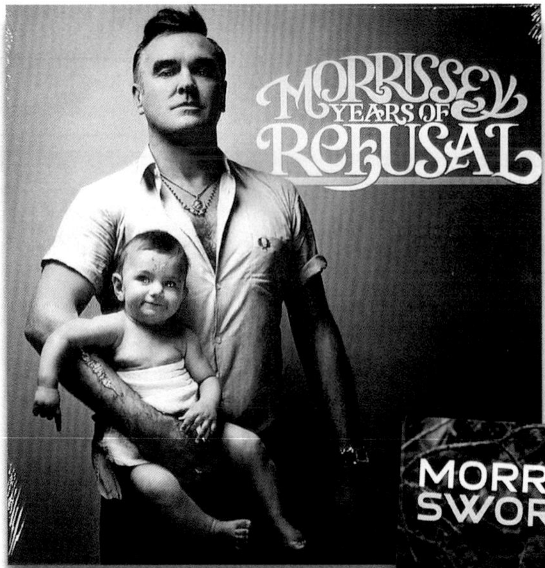

Left: Morrissey's ninth studio album, the last record produced by Jerry Finn before his death in 2008. Released in February 2009. (*Decca/BMG*)

Right: An incomplete compilation of B-sides taken from singles released 2004-2009, which came out in October 2009. (*Polydor/Universal*)

Left: Morrissey's deleted tenth studio album, released in July 2014, and withdrawn just three weeks later. (*Harvest/ Universal*)

Right: The new sleeve design for the deluxe edition of *Low in High School*, released in 2018. The album was originally released in 2017. *(Étienne/BMG)*

Left: Morrissey's album of cover versions, released in May 2019. *(Étienne/BMG)*

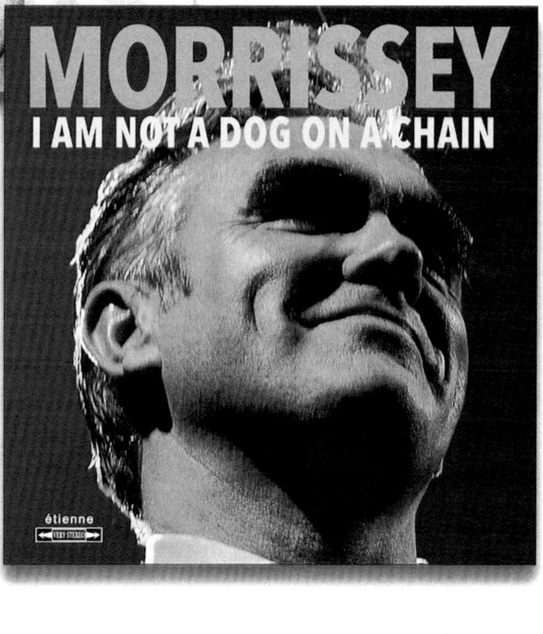

Right: Morrissey's 13th and latest solo album. Released in March 2020. *(BMG)*

Above: Morrissey performing live in 2019. (*photographer unknown*)

Left: The long-awaited autobiography, released as a *Penguin Classic* in October 2013. (*Penguin Books*)

was co-written with Street, just like most songs at this point. Musically, it's quite reminiscent of latter period Smiths, circa *Strangeways, Here We Come* (which came out just the year before), and there's also a not so discreet reference to 'How Soon Is Now?' in Vini Reilly's guitar, and the overall mood of the song. In the lyrics, Morrissey mocks himself in a way, as he sings about how lonely he is, drinking to make himself feel better, and finally promising that he will never sing again before he instantly changes his mind (thankfully). By the way, the shouting at the end of the song came from Reilly, Street, Andrew Paresi, and Steve Williams, who engineered the sessions.

'Happy Lovers at Last United' (Morrissey/Street)

The first of the unreleased bonus tracks on the 2010 reissue, this song was recorded during the 'Everyday Is Like Sunday' sessions in 1988 and was intended to be a B-side for that very single, but for some reason, Morrissey decided it wasn't good enough. And that's too bad, as it's not bad in any way. Street's tune is a good enough pop song, and Morrissey's lyrics are quite humorous, in a good way (as his 'funny' lyrics quite often are his weakest). Here we find him reuniting two friends who have recently split up and finally getting them back together, only to be pushed out of their life, as they don't really need him anymore.

'Lifeguard on Duty' (Morrissey/Street)

It's quite impossible not to draw comparisons to 'Lifeguard Sleeping, Girl Drowning' (from *Vauxhall And I*, 1994) when seeing this title, but this song, recorded during the *Viva Hate* sessions in 1987, is nothing like it. This was one of the first songs that Morrissey wrote with producer Stephen Street (who went on to write most of *Viva Hate*), and it's far from their best, which they probably felt at the time too. Street later recalled that they kept coming up with better songs for the album, which meant that this one went on the scrapheap. In the lyrics, Moz explains that he thinks that it sounds like the lifeguard by the pool has a much more important role than saving him from drowning but to save him from life itself.

'Please Help the Cause Against Loneliness' (Morrissey/Street)

This was originally intended to be recorded for the *Viva Hate* album, and Morrissey invited his idol, Sandie Shaw (who had previously recorded a few Smiths songs in the mid-80s), to sing backing vocals on it. In the end, he decided that he didn't want to use the song on the album anyway and instead offered it to Shaw, who recorded her version for the 1988 album *Hello Angel*. Morrissey later said that the song was frozen and that Shaw 'put it in the microwave'. Apart from being recorded in a different key, this version is similar to the one Shaw recorded (with the same musicians), and as her recording didn't even chart when it was released as a single, Moz probably made the right decision after all.

'Oh Phoney' (Morrissey/Armstrong)

This song was recorded for the proposed second album, *Bona Drag*, but as those sessions were aborted, as was this track. The standout line in the lyrics is probably: 'Who can make Hitler seem like a bus conductor? You do, Phoney, you do,' which he sings to another, unnamed singer. The acoustic song has a somewhat complex chord structure, especially in the chorus, where you sometimes wonder what the melody is. It was not really a potential track for a single, but a decent song anyway.

'The Bed Took Fire' (Morrissey/Street)

This song was later recorded with a new title, 'At Amber', for the B-side of 'Piccadilly Palare' in 1990, but this is the original demo version, recorded with co-writer Street in 1988. Back then, it was intended to be on the flip side of the 'Interesting Drug' single, until Morrissey changed his mind and the song ended up on the scrapheap. Then, a year later, while recording the second album, he decided that he wanted to bring this song back to life with the new title, 'At Amber'. So, Morrissey asked Street to join him, and his new producers Langer and Winstanley, in the studio to rearrange the song to suit the other recordings that they made for the album, an experience Street later said was quite uncomfortable, as he had an ongoing financial disagreement with Moz at this time. But he did this thing (making this new version much lighter and airier) and then went back home again. The lyrics are his first regarding a disabled person, who he's calling from a hotel to complain about what a terrible time he's having there.

'Let the Right One Slip In – Long Mix' (Morrissey/Whyte/Day)

For some odd reason, this song, recorded during the *Your Arsenal* sessions in 1992, was inserted as the last track on this reissue of *Bona Drag*, just like the regular version was included as a bonus track on the *Viva Hate* reissue in 2012. The song was written with Alain Whyte and Gary Day and was originally the B-side of 'Tomorrow' (1992), but with its big power chords and meandering guitar riff, it sounds like many of the other songs on Morrissey's third solo album. The title later influenced the title of Swedish author John Ajvide Lindqvist's novel *Låt den rätte komma in* (*Let the Right One In*), a book that was also made into a film in both Sweden and the US (*Let Me In*). Ajvide Lindqvist then released a collection of short stories entitled *Låt de gamla drömmarna dö*, (*Let The Old Dreams Die*) – the next line in the lyrics to the song.

Other Contemporary Songs

'Get off the Stage' (Morrissey/Rourke)

Another one of the more humorous Morrissey songs, in which he takes quite a few stabs at ageing rock stars. At the time, the song was aimed at Mick Jagger of The Rolling Stones, but I guess the lyrics are applicable to almost every rock star older than 50, really. Musically, the song features a lot of accordion, which is a rare instrument on Morrissey recordings, and we can also hear the Madness singer Graham 'Suggs' McPherson on backing vocals, having also sung on 'Piccadilly Palare', the A-side on the single from which this track comes.

Kill Uncle (1991)

Personnel:
Morrissey: vocals
Mark E Nevin: guitar
Mark Bedford: bass guitar
Andrew Paresi: drums, percussion
Seamus Beaghen: keyboards
Steven Heart: keyboards
Gino Sprio: sleeve photography
Jo Slee: art coordinator
Recorded at Hook End Manor
Produced by Clive Langer and Alan Winstanley
Playing time: 33:02
Label: HMV (UK), EMI (US)
Release date: March 4th 1991
Highest chart position: UK: 8

Morrissey's second solo album was released almost to the day three years after *Viva Hate,* and many fans would have surely wondered what had happened to him, as they would have been used to a quite furious release frequency. He had now chosen to leave Stephen Street behind and instead opted for the production duo Clive Langer and Alan Winstanley (who had produced bands like Madness, The Teardrop Explodes, Lloyd Cole & The Commotions and Aztec Camera), with Mark E Nevin (guitarist and songwriter for Fairground Attraction, who had a smash hit in 1988 with 'Perfect') writing most of the songs with Morrissey.

But the three-year gap wasn't intentional, and the plan was to release the second album, originally called *Bona Drag*, in early 1990, with the recordings going ahead as planned. Then Morrissey released the single 'Ouija Board, Ouija Board', which was slammed by more or less every music critic in the UK (it also did poorly in the charts), and he decided that he didn't want to go on with the album. He also got rid of his entire backing band (which by this time was most of his former Smiths bandmates, apart from Marr) and instead asked Paresi to once again take a seat behind the kit. He was then joined by Madness bassist Mark Bedford, guitarist Nevin, and the two keyboardists Seamus Beaghen (who had also played with Madness) and Steve Nieve (who was renamed Steve Heart on the sleeve, and a member of Elvis Costello's band The Attractions).

Kill Uncle is one of Morrissey's less popular albums among his fans, maybe in close competition with some of his latter-day efforts, the main reason probably being that it doesn't sound like the Morrissey we knew up until then. Langer and Winstanley really didn't want to copy The Smiths' sound, and therefore made it softer and lighter than what you might expect from Moz. Nevin also added a bit of the rockabilly influence that would come to full bloom within the next couple of years, most notably on 'Sing Your Life' and perhaps also on 'King Leer', if you accept a quite liberal definition of rockabilly. So, coupled with the piano-heavy arrangements, this wasn't your ordinary Morrissey outing.

In an interview with US radio station WDRE New York in November 1991, Morrissey described the album as 'just me and my views of life as I live it', while producer Langer later said that he thought the album was merely 'a bunch of poems stuck to music', and if you combine the two statements, you are actually getting quite close to the gist of *Kill Uncle.* That said, I think that it doesn't deserve its bad reputation, and there are some really good songs on it.

'Our Frank' (Morrissey/Nevin)

Released as the first single off the album, 'Our Frank' was also the first Morrissey/Nevin song officially released and the first track they recorded for the album. The humorous lyrics made both Nevin and Bedford laugh when they first heard them, and Morrissey himself has said that it's about being bored with friends who want to have deep conversations with him. The lines 'Our frank and open / Deep conversations / They get me nowhere / They bring me down, so give it a rest, won't you?' really says it all. The chorus also famously includes the lines about him throwing up all over his friend's red pullover. The music video made for the single, directed by John Maybury, was 'so awful that we tried to hide it', according to Morrissey. It was quite rare for many years, but it's now available on his own channel on YouTube, so I guess he changed his mind in the end.

'Asian Rut' (Morrissey/Nevin)

When non-Morrissey fans try to pin the 'racist' tag on him while looking at his song catalogue, this one often pops up– for no reason, really. They may have a point when talking about 'Bengali In Platforms' and 'National Front Disco' (from the *Your Arsenal* album), but in this song, Morrissey is rather telling a story about an Asian man trying to avenge the murder of his friend, a killing with racial motifs. The music was written by Nevin, and unlike the other demo recordings he sent to Morrissey, he actually gave this one a title, 'Idiot's Funeral', as he thought it had 'funereal qualities'. The sombre mood is enhanced by esteemed violinist Nawazish Ali Khan, and the song also features Roger Beaujolais (from Chevalier Brothers) on vibraphone, though the latter didn't get any credit on the album sleeve.

'Sing Your Life' (Morrissey/Nevin)

With Morrissey's imminent venture into rockabilly, this can surely be seen as the starting point of that change of sound, even though the production on this album version is far too airy for the song to be a real rockabilly track, and the use of keyboard strings (courtesy of Steve Nieve) also disqualifies it a bit. The song was released as the second single from the album, on April 1 1991, peaking at #33 in the UK, making it Morrissey's lowest charting single thus far, and also features Madness singer Suggs on backing vocals (the B-side, a cover version of The Jam's 'That's Entertainment' featured Madness' other vocalist, Chas Smash, on backing vocals). Lyrically, this is a fairly straightforward one, with Morrissey telling his audience to believe in themselves and start making music of their own ('Sing your life / Any fool can think of words that rhyme / Many others do, why don't you? / Do you want to? /... / Just walk right up to the microphone and name / All the things you love / All the things you loathe'). A call to arms, so to speak. The music video, filmed with most of Morrissey's new backing band (apart from guitarist Boz Boorer), also stars Chrissie Hynde (of The Pretenders), dancing among all the rockabilly kids at the replica of a 1950s club.

'Mute Witness' (Morrissey/Langer)

After singing about murderous revenge on 'Asian Rut', Morrissey here conjures the image of a mute girl trying to make a witness statement to the police but sadly failing, with the song ending on the sad note: 'It could have been so clear / If only she had never volunteered / 'Your taxi is here, my dear'.' The singer is clearly attempting to find this whole story rather amusing, which threatens to leave a bitter taste in the mouth. The piano intro is quite reminiscent of the US duo Sparks – their biggest hit 'This Town Ain't Big Enough For Both of Us' in particular) – and Roxy Music, an influence that producer Langer also admitted to later. Langer co-wrote the song with Morrissey, and played the guitar solo.

'King Leer' (Morrissey/Nevin)

Well, I think we can agree on the fact that Morrissey's humorous lyrics aren't always his most beloved ones (even though they can be good), and this one is probably one of his least liked, as is the song. All the people involved in its making have later said that they don't know why it was included on the album, apart from Morrissey himself, who at one point claimed that it was his favourite track on the record. And sure, if you hear the live version played by his rockabilly influenced band on the *Kill Uncle* tour, it sounds like a funny, stompy tune. But on the album, Morrissey's description of the song having 'a very English tearoom feel' is more than true. The title is, of course, a play on Shakespeare's play 'King Lear'.

'Found Found Found' (Morrissey/Langer)

Another one of the songs Morrissey co-wrote with Langer, this is the album's rocker, if you might call it that, and indeed Langer claims that he wrote the music for it after the singer requested a 'punk song', and then knocked it out in five minutes. In the early 90s, there was a rumour that the lyrics were about Michael Stipe (of R.E.M.), who became friends with Morrissey at about that time, but the song is really about the fact that you either find your friends yourself or they find you.

'Driving Your Girlfriend Home' (Morrissey/Nevin)

Easily my favourite track on *Kill Uncle*, and actually one of my favourites among Morrissey's entire solo catalogue, this is yet another song concerning two people riding a car together, with a hint of unrequited love in the air– a theme Morrissey previously dealt with on 'This Charming Man' and 'There's a Light That Never Goes Out'. The backing vocals were provided by Moz's friend Linder Sterling (a founding member of post-punk outfit Ludus, and also an artist and photographer), and it's been suggested through the years that the lyrics are actually about her. Musically, it's as soft as lace, with stand-up bass being quite prominent throughout the song.

'The Harsh Truth of the Camera Eye' (Morrissey/Nevin)

By far the longest song on the album at 5:34, the producers obviously realised that the song needed something 'extra', so the recording was spiced up with various sound effects (screams, camera noises, a skateboard rolling from speaker to speaker etc.). So, what is the song about, then? Well, it's about the uncomfortable feeling that you can get when being photographed when you might not want to. It's hardly anyone's favourite song on the album.

'(I'm) The End of the Family Line' (Morrissey/Nevin)

'I can't imagine anything as terrible as little Morrisseys running around below the plum tree in my kitchen garden', Morrissey told Swedish journalist Andres Lokko in 1992, and even though he might have been joking, there was a glimpse of truth in that statement. Already on The Smiths song 'Stretch Out and Wait', he asked 'is there any point ever having children?', and during the years between the two songs, he seemed to have made up his mind. Many of the musicians on the album have said that this is their favourite song on it, and it's really not bad. And by the way – he's not the end of his family line, as his sister Jackie had two sons, Sam and Johnny, who are both working in the music industry (Sam Esty Rayner starred in the music video for 'Suedehead', and also directed the dubious video for 'Kiss Me A Lot' in 2015).

'There's a Place in Hell for Me and My Friends' (Morrissey/Nevin)

The album closer is something of a hymn, where Morrissey imagines an afterlife spent in flames, rather than among the clouds. The backing track is really simple, with just a piano and some strings, and the piano that can be heard on the album is actually taken from the demo that Nevin recorded for Morrissey. He later explained that they tried to re-record the piano part in the studio but never quite nailed it, so they decided to go with the home recording instead. For the 2013 reissue, the original album version was replaced by one recorded 'live in the studio', which was actually first released as a B-side to 'My Love Life' in September 1991, and uses guitars instead of the gentle piano, which makes it 'rockier'.

Other Contemporary Songs

'Tony the Pony' (Morrissey/Nevin)

This song, released as a B-side on the 'Our Frank' 12' single, was added to the US release of the album by Sire for some reason, and they apparently didn't check with Morrissey first. He actually considered including it on the album, but he changed his mind, as he thought that it sounded too much like something he had heard before (according to drummer Paresi). The song fits somewhere in between the classic pop sound and the rockabilly influences that gradually made their way into Morrissey's music at this time. The 'Tony' in the song is allegedly an older brother who keeps a close watch on his younger sibling, to the latter's annoyance.

'Pashernate Love' (Morrissey/Whyte/Day)

On the 2013 expanded reissue, two songs have been added to the tracklist, thrown in among the original songs, the first one being this one, originally released as the B-side to the single 'You're the One For Me, Fatty', in July 1992. It might seem like an odd choice to include a song from the *Your Arsenal* era on *Kill Uncle*, but since the band started playing it live on the tour following the latter album, it perhaps made sense, at least to Morrissey. This was one of the first songs written by Moz's new guitarist Alain Whyte (who actually co-wrote it with bassist Gary Day) that was recorded, and in its lyrics, Morrissey talks about passionate love being something of a mystery to him.

'East West' (Graham Gouldman)

(see 'Ouija Board, Ouija Board' single)

'Journalists Who Lie' (Morrissey/Street)

This B-side of 'Our Frank' was one of the first songs the band recorded for *Kill Uncle* in 1991, but Morrissey decided to omit it from the album in the end, and that was certainly for the best. It's quite a horrible song, to be honest, and that owes a lot to the weird production by Langer and Winstanley. The song really wants to be a rockabilly rocker, but as they have thrown in synthesizers and odd sound effects, it just sounds schizophrenic. This was the final song written with Stephen Street that was released, but he's not playing on it (nor producing it, sadly). And the lyrics? Well, do I really have to tell you what they are about?

'That's Entertainment' (Paul Weller)

This cover of The Jam's classic song (originally appearing on their *Sound Affects* album in 1980) was recorded at the end of the sessions for *Kill Uncle*, and later appeared as a B-side to the 'Sing Your Life' single in 1991. Morrissey wanted to put his own stamp on the rendition, so he decided to make it an acoustic affair, with Cathal Smyth (also known as Chas Smash) from Madness singing backing vocals, while Kate St John (who was once a member of

The Dream Academy) stopped by to play some woodwind. The sleeve also credits comedian Vic Reeves (or Jim Moir, which is his real name), but his contributions to the finished song remain a bit unclear. It's also unclear as to why the song begins and ends with the sound of a distant stream train.

'There Speaks a True Friend' (Morrissey/Whyte)

Originally released as a B-side to 'You're the One for Me, Fatty' in 1992, this song is about saying goodbye to a friend who told him all the things that are wrong with him, but walked away before the singer had a chance to put them right. It starts out sounding a bit like Madness in their poppier days, but the most memorable thing about this tune is probably the odd ending, where the song suddenly cuts off, which was allegedly Moz's idea, as he didn't like the original outro, which was much longer.

Contemporary Singles

Pregnant for the Last Time (single, 1991)

Personnel:
Morrissey: vocals
Mark Nevin: guitars
Boz Boorer: guitars
Jonny Bridgwood: bass guitar
Andrew Paresi: drums

'Pregnant for the Last Time' (Morrissey/Nevin)

This is one of the less successful Morrissey singles of the 90s (released on July 15 1991, peaking at #25 in the UK), so I often feel alone in thinking that this is a great song. It was written with Mark Nevin – who Morrissey had worked with on the *Kill Uncle* album – and was recorded as part of a planned rockabilly mini-album that Moz wanted to make with his new band (Boorer, Alain Whyte and Jonny Bridgwood). However, this song was the only one that was finished. Whyte originally played the harmonica on the track, but his contributions never made it to the final mix. This foot-stamping rockabilly rocker was even more fierce when played live, with double bass and a much faster tempo (have a look at the live video *Live in Dallas* or listen to the B-side of the 'We Hate It When Our Friends Become Successful' 12' single, for example). The lyrics are a tip of the hat to single mothers who keep ending up in new relationships and then getting pregnant (for the last time), with the doctor telling the mother not to nod her head until June and being sick at noon (for the last time).

'Skin Storm' (Ian Michael Hodgson)

This song was originally recorded by the band Bradford, and it was their debut single in 1988 on the small indie label Village Records– it was allegedly the first indie single released on CD. Morrissey's version is very similar to the original recording, and since singer Ian Hodgson was clearly influenced by Moz, it's quite hard to hear the difference, initially. Bradford also opened for Morrissey at his much anticipated first solo concert in Wolverhampton in 1988.

'Cosmic Dancer (live)' (Marc Bolan)
Recorded live in Utrecht, The Netherlands, on May 1 1991, this is Morrissey's acoustic rendition of the T Rex classic, originally released on the *Electric Warrior* album in 1971. Moz was inspired to cover the song after watching the concert film *Born To Boogie* (1972, directed by Ringo Starr), where Bolan performed the song in the same way as Morrissey and Boorer do on this recording, and he then sang it as an encore during the *Kill Uncle* tour. A version recorded with David Bowie in Los Angeles a month later was released as a 7' single in 2020.

'Disappointed (live)' (Morrissey/Street)
This live version of a B-side of 'Everyday Is Like Sunday' was recorded during the same show as 'Cosmic Dancer', and features Morrissey getting interrupted by fans invading the stage (one of them screaming 'Morrissey!' into the microphone).

My Love Life (single, 1991)

Personnel:
Morrissey: vocals
Mark Nevin: guitars
Mark Bedford: bass guitar
Andrew Paresi: drums
Chrissie Hynde: backing vocals

'My Love Life' (Morrissey/Nevin)
Released as Morrissey's eleventh solo single on September 17, 1991, (peaking at #29), it was a non-album release, which came out between *Kill Uncle* and *Your Arsenal*. It was recorded during the sessions for the former album but, on the sleeve, the band is incorrectly listed as being the one on the latter. The song was written with Mark Nevin, and was originally considered to be a B-side, but then Moz decided to release it as a standalone single instead, especially after Chrissie Hynde (of The Pretenders) joined in on backing vocals. The jangly, poppy sound doesn't really sound like the rest of *Kill Uncle,* so Morrissey was already moving away from the rockabilly influences when he recorded this plea for being part of a polyamorous relation. The song was available in two versions, one for the UK and for the US, where the latter is 25 seconds longer.

'I've Changed My Plea to Guilty' (Morrissey/Nevin)
After recording this song, Morrissey said that this was the best one he had ever recorded. Despite that, it ended up on a B-side, even though it would have

been a great addition to the *Kill Uncle* album. This impassioned piano ballad is great in its simplicity, as it's just Morrissey and Nevin's piano, and the vocals are truly amazing, with the high notes on 'freedom is wasted on me' acting as a great example of the singer's vocal range. The sounds in the intro and the outro are sampled from 'The End of the World', Skeeter Davis' hit single from 1963, and also from some recordings that a waitress friend of Nevin did at her workplace. Both these samples were omitted on the US version of the single, for some reason, which instead has the full piano outro. When played live, the song was rearranged to suit the stage setup and was therefore played on guitar instead of piano, which sadly made the song lose much of its charm.

'There's a Place in Hell for Me and My Friends' (Morrissey/ Nevin)

Just like 'I've Changed My Plea to Guilty', this song also got the rock treatment when performed live, and once again, a lovely piano ballad lost its charm. This version was recorded during a live session for US radio station *KROQ* on June 3 1991, and the complete three-song session (with 'My Love Life' and 'Sing Your Life') was released as a US-only CD single called *Morrissey at KROQ* later that year.

Your Arsenal (1992)

Personnel:
Morrissey: vocals
Boz Boorer: guitars
Alain Whyte: guitars
Gary Day: bass guitar
Spencer Cobrin: drums
Linder Sterling: sleeve photography
E Riff: sleeve
Jo Slee: sleeve
Designland: sleeve
Recorded at Utopia Studios, The Wool Hall
Produced by Mick Ronson
Playing time: 39 min 45 sec
Label: HMV (UK), EMI (US)
Release date: July 27 1992
Highest chart position: UK: 4

After finishing the recording sessions for *Kill Uncle*, Morrissey set out to find himself a new live band for the upcoming tour and soon found guitarist Boz Boorer (real name Martin James Boorer), a former member of rockabilly revivalists The Polecats, who released a bunch of records in the early 80s and also managed to score some minor hits both in the UK and the US. He was then joined by another guitarist, Alain Whyte, who had already been seen in the music video for 'Sing Your Life', together with former guitarist Mark Nevin, (who was unable to join them on tour, but still supplied two songs for the album), bass player Gary Day, who first joined Team Morrissey back in 1990, but didn't play on *Kill Uncle*, and drummer Spencer Cobrin. Whyte, Day and Cobrin already played together as rockabilly act The Memphis Sinners, so together with Boorer, that band became Morrissey's new band, with Whyte as the main songwriter and Boorer as their musical director.

Apart from Boorer, none of the other band members had any previous experience of recording in a studio, so the sessions in Utopia (where two songs were recorded) and The Wool Hall (where The Smiths recorded *Strangeways, Here We Come* and *Viva Hate*), soon became something of a youth centre, with a bunch of twenty-year-old guys passing the time with all kinds of mischief. But that didn't stop them from making a great record – a record that would be a comeback of sorts for Morrissey, even though the previous album had been released just a year earlier.

With Whyte as the main songwriter (much to Nevin's dismay, as he still considered himself to be the 'staff writer' before he realized that there was a new kid in town), and the rockabilly history of the band, the new songs swiftly changed Morrissey's musical course – away from the various experiments in different styles of the first two outings, to find a more solid and homogenous sound – even though there was still room for trying new things every now and then. And this new, rockier sound, would actually be more or less synonymous with Morrissey's forthcoming solo albums; and with Boorer as the sole 'surviving' band member to this day, he has made sure that the legacy lives on.

Then they had to find a producer, as Langer and Winstanley were out of the picture at this time. Nevin suggested John Cale, former member of The Velvet Underground, and also a producer of Patti Smith's classic album 'Horses' (among others), but he was unavailable, so Morrissey suggested Tony Visconti (who produced albums by T Rex and David Bowie), who also turned down the offer. At last, they settled for Mick Ronson, who played guitar with Bowie as a member of The Spiders from Mars during the Ziggy Stardust period, and then kept collaborating with Bowie and many other associated artists in the future. As the band was leaning towards a rockier sound, the choice of Ronson, with his roots in the glam rock scene, was a perfect one, and he definitely made the album stand out in the Morrissey catalogue.

The sleeve, which was made by E. Riff, according to the sleeve notes (but that was of course yet another one of Morrissey's pseudonyms), boasts a photo of Morrissey, taken by Linder Sterling (remember her from 'Driving Your Girlfriend Home'?) at an earlier concert.

The album was praised more or less universally by critics, and it peaked at number four on the UK albums chart. Most critics saw this as a new awakening for Morrissey, and it would turn out that they were right.

'You're Gonna Need Someone on Your Side' (Morrissey/Nevin)

Despite being out of the picture at the time of the album's recording, Nevin still had two songs included on the record – the lovely 'I Know It's Gonna Happen Someday', and this smoking opener, which was the perfect introduction to the new and improved Morrissey. Nevin wrote the song at the same time as two other songs in the same vein, 'Pregnant for the Last Time', and the instrumental 'The Loop', which were all supposed to be included on a planned mini-album of rockabilly songs. That never happened, and instead, Morrissey's new backing band took over the song and turned it into a riff-laden rocker. In the lyrics, Moz tackles the need for friends to rely on, a theme that would return on his next album ('Hold On to Your Friends' on *Vauxhall and I*).

'Glamorous Glue' (Morrissey/Whyte)

Almost seamlessly crossfading from the previous song, 'Glamorous Glue' is yet another rocker, though far less energetic. This one was written with new songwriting partner Alain Whyte, and it's fair to say that Ronson's background in Bowie's band is rather audible on this song, which also boasts a slide guitar solo courtesy of Boz Boorer. A music video for the song was made at the time of the album's release, but it wouldn't be until 2011 that the track had its deserved single release (to promote the compilation album *The Very Best of*

Morrissey). And no, the title is not referring to the adhesive qualities of glue, but rather as a description of how people in Thatcher's Britain escaped the dullness of reality. Morrissey also finds the time to criticize the UK for being too influenced by the US in general, and Los Angeles in particular, exclaiming that 'London is dead!'

'We'll Let You Know' (Morrissey/Whyte)

This is as close as we get to a title track on this album (the mob that can be heard in the song shouts 'Your Arsenal!' somewhere in the middle), and after two foot-stomping tracks, things are slowing down a bit here, with acoustic guitars at the centre of attention instead of riffing electric ones. Morrissey has repeatedly said that this song is one of his favourites among his recorded output, which is stretching it a bit far. And considering the allegations of nationalism, the lyrics, which can easily be interpreted as a tribute to the English football hooligans that shook the world back in those days (and sadly still do from time to time), do leave a slightly bitter aftertaste in your mouth. But I can't deny that it's still a great song.

'National Front Disco' (Morrissey/Whyte)

So, we have come to this, then: one of the most controversial songs in the Morrissey songbook, and as you might have guessed by now – there are a few of those. And if the title wasn't enough, Morrissey made a habit of draping himself in the Union Jack (the UK flag) while playing this live on the *Your Arsenal* tour. But let's start from the beginning. After reading Bill Buford's book *Among the Thugs* (1991), in which the author investigated and exposed the British football hooligan, and spent a full chapter on telling the story about a group of skinheads who attended a National Front disco, Morrissey wrote this song, which focuses on a guy called David, who is lost to the National Front. Sadly, many people didn't realise that the exclamation 'England for the English!' was actually a quote, and not Morrissey using the old National Front slogan for showcasing his own beliefs. In the light of his statements regarding the state of the UK during the past decade or so, it does feel a bit prescient. Despite this controversy, Morrissey opted to include the song in his live sets well into the 2010s.

'Certain People I Know' (Morrissey/Whyte)

For the first time on this album, we're heading into Rockabilly Land, and this time Whyte took the T Rex classic 'Ride a White Swan' and rewrote it slightly, probably to avoid being sued for plagiarism. That didn't stop most critics and fans from spotting the obvious resemblance, and even Morrissey himself eventually introduced the song as 'Certain White Swans I Know' when playing it live. The song was released as the fourth single from the album in December 1992, and peaked at #35 in the UK singles chart. The single was originally planned to have Morrissey's name spelt out in the colours of the Union Jack flag, but after the controversies surrounding 'National Front Disco', the label decided to go with black letters instead. The lyrics are self-explanatory, and I guess a lot of people in Morrissey's circle of friends may have wondered whether the song was about them or not.

'We Hate It When Our Friends Become Successful' (Morrissey/Whyte)

The third song on the album dealing with friends in one way or another, and yet another rather self-explanatory title. This was the first single to be released from *Your Arsenal*, in April 1992 (peaking at #17 in the UK). Morrissey himself has said that it was about the menacing competition in Manchester, where, according to him, success is frowned upon. It was later suggested that the lyrics were in fact aimed at Manchester band, James (who scored a few hits in the UK in the early 90s, with 'Sit Down' probably being the one people most remember), and their lead singer Tim Booth in particular; both parties have more or less confirmed this in their own ways. This was the first song written by Whyte that was performed on stage by Morrissey, as they introduced it in the live set during the second half of the *Kill Uncle* tour in late 1991. I also recommend having a look at the music video made for the song, directed by Tim Broad, where Moz and the boys in the band play around in a rowdy backyard, looking like a gang of hoodlums – with the star of the show being drummer Spencer Cobrin, who tries to seduce Morrissey with a Cornetto ice cream cone. The bonus tracks on the single consisted of live versions of 'Suedehead', 'I've Changed My Plea to Guilty', 'Alsatian Cousin', and 'Pregnant for The Last Time', all recorded in London in 1991.

'You're the One for Me, Fatty' (Morrissey/Whyte)

The second single to be released from the album, in July 1992, peaking at #19 in the UK. Most fans probably took the lyrics at face value, interpreting it as a love song to an overweight person (Morrissey's friend Kirsty MacColl was often considered the subject), which was also the theme of the music video that was made for the single. But in fact, it was a song written for a certain person, namely Chas Smash of Madness, who became friends with Morrissey in the early 90s, with both of them confirming him as the subject later on. Musically, it's more reminiscent of The Smiths and *Viva Hate* than the 'new and improved' Morrissey, with its jangly guitars and pop melody, which might also explain why the single broke the top 20 in the singles chart.

'Seasick, Yet Still Docked' (Morrissey/Whyte)

Songwriter Alain Whyte once admitted in an interview that this song was written to sound like a Smiths tune, and it succeeds quite well, with the waltz-esque tempo sounding a bit like 'That Joke Isn't Funny Anymore', and the band version of 'Back to the Old House'. The lyrics are written from an older man's point of view, looking back on a life that didn't quite go as planned, with the ticking clock featured in the beginning and the end of the song marking the time passing.

'I Know It's Gonna Happen Someday' (Morrissey/Nevin)
Time for Mark Nevin's second contribution to this album, and musically this one is as far from the first one as possible. Where 'You're Gonna Need Someone on Your Side' was a rockabilly romper, he went for a ballad for his next tune, one that impressed Morrissey so much in its demo version (where it was called 'French Epic'), that he exclaimed that it was Nevin's best song. The version on the album still features all the various radio noises that Nevin put on his demo, and the song then ends with a more or less intended tribute to David Bowie's 'Rock'n'roll Suicide' (which Ronson played on). How fitting then that Bowie himself would record a cover of this song for his *Black Tie, White Noise* album the following year, where he omitted the tribute ending. As you might have noticed by now, the yearning for love is never far away in Morrissey's lyrics, and this is yet another one of those songs; but this one is a bit more optimistic than usual (as the title suggests), as the crooning singer pleads for the person not to lose faith.

'Tomorrow' (Morrissey/Whyte)
Many fans listening to the album for the first time probably expected it to end with the powerful ballad above, but they were in for one last treat. 'Tomorrow' was written by Whyte and was never released as a single in the UK, but it did get a US release in September 1992 (with a cover photo that preceded the song 'The Lazy Sunbathers' on his next album), where it actually ended up topping *Billboard*'s Hot Modern Rock Tracks chart. The music video shows Morrissey walking through the back streets of Nice (France), while his band is following behind him, mucking about. Lyrically, he once again returns to yearning for love, or rather getting a hug to make his 'shiftless body' less shiftless. By the way, doesn't the piano at the end of the song sound a lot like 'Asleep'?

Other Contemporary Tracks

'You've Had Her' (Morrissey/Boorer)
This B-side to 'Certain People I Know' was one of the first songs Morrissey wrote with new guitarist Boz Boorer (who's still working with Moz at the time of writing). It's quite far from his best contribution to this catalogue, with mainly just the guitar and a howling wind accompanying Morrissey while he sings about how womanizers don't care about the women they chat up.

Beethoven Was Deaf (live album, 1993)

Personnel:
Morrissey: vocals
Boz Boorer: guitars
Alain Whyte: guitars, backing vocals
Gary Day: bass guitar, double bass
Spencer Cobrin: drums
Whores In Retirement: sleeve
Linder Sterling: photography
Mixed by Bob Clearmountain
Playing time: 61:05
Label: HMV (UK)
Release date: May 10th 1993
Highest chart position: UK: 13

1993 was a quiet year for Morrissey, in between his two albums *Your Arsenal* and *Vauxhall And I,* so to keep up momentum, his first solo live album was released, mostly to show the world what a great backing band he had now, and that they were a fierce live act. Listening to the album, there's no doubt about that. So, I guess it was mission accomplished. According to the sleeve, the album was recorded at the Zenith in Paris, France on December 22nd 1992, but the truth is that half of the songs here were recorded at the Astoria in London on December 21st.

The songs are mostly taken from the latest album at the time, *Your Arsenal*, which isn't that strange, really, as this live band played on that record as well. But played live, many of the songs are indeed a lot rockier and faster, and some of the older tracks have been 'rockabilly-fied'. At this point in his career, Morrissey refused to play Smiths songs in his live shows, so there are none here.

In 2010, EMI announced that this album was deleted from their catalogue as a physical release, which means that you can no longer get hold of it, unless you can find a second hand copy, though it is still available on the major streaming sites.

Vauxhall and I (1994)

Personnel:
Morrissey: vocals
Boz Boorer: guitars
Alain Whyte: guitars
Jonny Bridgwood: bass guitar
Woodie Taylor: drums
Dean Freeman: photography
Recorded at Hook End Manor
Produced by Steve Lillywhite
Playing time: 39:53
Label: Parlophone (UK), Sire/Reprise (US)
Release date: March 14 1994
Highest chart position: UK: 1, US: 18

After being re-ignited on *Your Arsenal*, Morrissey was on a roll and wanted to quickly begin working on the follow-up album. But then suddenly, three friends of his passed away (manager Nigel Thomas, video director Tim Broad, and producer Mick Ronson), which made him isolate himself in his Camden house; he didn't emerge until mid-1993 when the recording sessions for his fourth solo album finally took off.

Morrissey decided to stick with Alain Whyte and Boz Boorer as his guitarists, but he felt that Spencer Cobrin and Gary Day weren't quite living up to his expectations as band members, so he asked Boorer to find their replacements. Soon they were instead joined by bass player Jonny Bridgwood (who had played with Boz in the band Boz and the Bozmen, and also in psychobilly band The Sting-Rays) and drummer Woodie Taylor (who was a member of The Meteors in the late 80s, and a future member of indie-pop punksters Comet Gain).

Morrissey had asked Ronson to produce the next album as well, but as he passed away from liver cancer in April 1993, Boorer asked his friend Steve Lillywhite to step in as producer instead (Lillywhite also worked with The Smiths when he remixed 'Ask' in 1986). This change of producer also meant that the sound moved away from the rock of *Your Arsenal* and instead became far more pop orientated, forming a new, softer sound that would essentially be the one that Morrissey would stick to in the future (apart from a few exceptions every now and then).

Where Whyte had been more or less the sole songwriter for *Your Arsenal* (apart from the two songs by Mark Nevin), Boorer now also wanted to contribute to the songs music-wise, which meant that Morrissey suddenly had two great songwriters competing for slots on the album. And maybe that competition was what made the album so great. Because great it is – quite possibly Morrissey's best solo album, an opinion I'm far from alone in having. *Vauxhall and I* also debuted in the UK album charts at number one, which hadn't happened since *Viva Hate* in 1988. For some reason, Morrissey decided not to tour in support of the album, so the songs had to wait to get live renditions until 1995's *Southpaw Grammar* tour.

The album was originally intended to be released in late 1993, but since Warner was about to re-release the entire Smiths catalogue at that time, Parlophone and Morrissey decided to push the release date until March 1994, which was probably a wise decision, as it's not hard to imagine that the singer got some new fans when his former band's albums were made available on CD.

'Now My Heart Is Full' (Morrissey/Boorer)

The album kicks off with Morrissey's farewell to his childhood, waving goodbye to all his old movie favourites, including the reference to the lead characters in Graham Greene's *Brighton Rock* (Dallow, Spicer, Pinkie and Cubitt), and Patric Doonan, who starred in *The Blue Lamp* (1950) and *Wheel Of Fate* (1953), among others. In an interview with the French music magazine *Les Inrockuptibles* in 1995, Morrissey said that he really enjoyed singing the lyrics to this song: 'after this song, I could perfectly retire – I've come full circle', which shows that he needed to address those childhood obsessions one last time to be able to move on.

The song starts off with just a slow, distorted guitar that paves the way to the chorus. The song was actually slower in its demo stage, before the band entered the studio with Lillywhite, when they instead opted to play it as they did in concert, which was a bit faster. But the bass part that can be heard on the album is actually taken from Boz's original demo, as bass player Bridgwood never really got it right in the studio.

The song was intended for single release, but it was eventually replaced by 'Hold on to Your Friends' in the UK. It did come out in the US but didn't make much of a fuss on the charts.

'Spring-Heeled Jim' (Morrissey/Boorer)

One of the first songs recorded for the album, this is yet another of Morrissey's 'character songs' (it's actually followed by another one, 'Billy Budd'), and another chance for him to indulge with thugs and other outcasts. The 'Jim' in this song is living life at five times the average speed, with a lot of alcohol and violence, and ends up spending his life alone. In the late 19th century, there was such a man, who terrorised London and the UK, called Spring-Heeled Jack, and this might have been the inspiration for this song, but Morrissey has never confirmed this. Throughout the song, you can hear some teenagers discussing a fight between some men and also the death penalty, taken from a documentary called *We Are the Lambeth Boys* (Karel Reisz, 1958).

'Billy Budd' (Morrissey/Whyte)

As I mentioned in the section about 'Spring-Heeled Jim' above, this is the album's second 'character song', but it isn't, in fact, about the persona of the same name in Herman Melville's short story (and the movie from 1960) – Morrissey is just using it as a nickname for a longtime friend. Who this friend might be has been up for discussion since the album came out, and for many, Johnny Marr seems like the obvious choice for various reasons. Just like the previous song, 'Billy Budd' features a sound clip from a movie, and this time it's from *Oliver Twist* (David Lean, 1948), from where Morrissey borrowed the line 'don't leave us in the dark', which ends the song. Musically, 'Billy Budd' is a step back to the rockier sound of *Your Arsenal*, and it's actually the only track in that vein on the album. As his backing band often preferred to make the live arrangements of the songs more 'muscular', this one quickly became a live favourite, as most of the other songs on the album never quite turned out great in that setting.

'Hold on to Your Friends' (Morrissey/Whyte)
Released as the second single from the album in May 1994, it peaked at #47 in the UK singles chart, which was a disappointment, considering the success of the album. Perhaps one of the reasons was that there was no music video made for it, in a time when MTV and other TV channels made all the difference for singles sales. As for the lyrics, Morrissey said at the time of the release that 'it was written about somebody I know in relation to their treatment toward me', a 'somebody' who betrayed the singer and therefore ended yet another of his close friendships. Recording engineer Chris Dickie told author Simon Goddard that Whyte's guitar melody was recorded note for note on separate tracks, which took a lot of time, and then they had to re-record it in the end when they realised that it was recorded in the wrong key…

'The More You Ignore Me, The Closer I Get' (Morrissey/Boorer)
In early 1994, Morrissey hadn't had a top ten single since 'Interesting Drug' in 1989, but things were about to change! This Boorer composition, actually the first single to be released with that writing credit, was originally slower and heavier until producer Lillywhite decided to turn it into a lovely, and far lighter pop song. It's actually the only Morrissey single to end up on the *Billboard* Hot 100 in the US (peaking at #46), and was also something of a smash hit in Iceland, where it stayed at #2 for three weeks! Lyrically, it's interesting to hear Morrissey singing about high court judges and declaring war on the subject of the song, bearing in mind the trials with Mike Joyce a few years later. The lamp heavy music video for the song was directed by Mark Romanek, who later directed the iconic video for Johnny Cash's 'Hurt' (2002), and also the movies *One Hour Photo* (2002) and *Never Let Me Go* (2010).

'Why Don't You Find Out for Yourself' (Morrissey/Whyte)
Another Whyte song, and another stab at the ruthlessness of the music industry from Morrissey (see Smiths song 'Paint a Vulgar Picture'), with lines about being stabbed in the back and being sucked dry economically. Whyte's

original demo was actually a lot rockier, and it was recorded as such too, when Lillywhite decided to make it a lot softer, with an acoustic guitar playing lead. But as he didn't want to start from the beginning with the song again, he kept Morrissey's vocal take and just made the band re-record the music. Oh, and listen for the rattling teacups in the background throughout the song (courtesy of Boorer)!

'I Am Hated for Loving' (Morrissey/Whyte)

In what seems to be a theme for this album, this song also started out as a rock song before the band decided to turn it down a notch in favour of strummed acoustic guitars and jangling electric guitars, not sounding too far off the old Smiths sound. Speaking to author Johnny Rogan, bass player Bridgwood said that he plays a Hofner violin bass (like Paul McCartney in The Beatles) on the track, which creates a bass sound that is a bit unusual for the album, and that drummer Taylor recorded his drums in the control room, playing them with brushes. The title itself is almost a Morrissey cliché, much in the tradition of songs like 'Heaven Knows I'm Miserable Now' and 'Unloveable', but it's a really beautiful song, and one of the best from the album.

'Lifeguard Sleeping, Girl Drowning' (Morrissey/Boorer)

This thrillingly atmospheric song, about a lifeguard ignoring a swimming girl's cries for help while he rests, is the odd one out on this album. Morrissey's whispered vocals and Boorer's clarinet-heavy arrangement is very fitting for the theme of the song, and Moz reportedly spent a lot of time getting the vocals right in the studio, which isn't hard to imagine. The repeated sample of 'What's your name?' at the end of the song is taken from the movie *In Which We Serve* (1942), which was written and co-directed by Morrissey's old favourite, Noël Coward.

'Used To Be a Sweet Boy' (Morrissey/Whyte)

Looking back on Morrissey's back catalogue, it's not very uncommon to find lyrics about his unfortunate youth and his dabblings in romance, but this was the first time he wrote anything about his parents. The lyrics are written from both his own perspective and his father's, where the line 'I'm not to blame' represents the parent saying that it's not his fault that his son turned out the way he did. He later said in interviews that he really did think that parents do have a big responsibility for their kids: 'they bring the children up, not the other way around.' Musically, the waltz-like melody is dominated once again by acoustic guitars and piano, both played by songwriter Whyte.

'The Lazy Sunbathers' (Morrissey/Whyte)

You can almost imagine an old yellowing postcard picturing a bunch of sunbathers on the English seaside when listening to this song, and contrary to 'popular' belief, it's not a tribute to ukulele man George Formby (which author Simon Goddard discusses in his great *Mozipedia* book). No, this one is rather about those who have and those who have not, where the former really doesn't care what happens to the latter, which is made all too obvious in the final lines: children are being bombed and the sunbathers are asking them to keep the noise down. Whyte's music is carried by a slow, jangly guitar line, but despite the overall feeling of a quite simple song, it was hard for the band to get it right when recording it in the studio, and in the end, Morrissey had to sing a guide vocal for them, which obviously did the trick!

'Speedway' (Morrissey/Boorer)

The closing track of this marvellous album also has one of the most powerful intros, as it opens with just Morrissey and an electric guitar before a drill (or is it a chainsaw?) interrupts and invites the whole band to the party. The song itself can be described as both a confession and an attack on his antagonists, as they try to pin various views and statements on him. A lot of people have been putting a lot of attention on the lines: 'all of the rumours / Keeping my grounded / I never said that they were completely unfounded,' and interpreting them as Morrissey confessing to being a racist, especially as the song was written after the 'National Front Disco' debate. He has indeed said in interviews that the lyrics might be him confessing that the rumours about him might not be all wrong, but that doesn't necessarily mean that everything is true. The drums at the end were recorded in the dining room at the studio, as they thought that the acoustics there were interesting, and it does sound bombastic, to say the least! A smashing end to a smashing album!

Other Contemporary Songs

'I'd Love To' (Morrissey/Boorer)

Originally released as a B-side to 'The More You Ignore Me, The Closer I Get' in 1994, this sweeping piano ballad is available in two versions, one made for the UK and one for the US (the latter, which features a few less guitars than the UK mix, was later included on the US only *My Early Burglary Years* compilation in 1998). The lyrics are classic Morrissey, full of self-pity, with the singer crying and mourning for love.

Contemporary Singles

Interlude (single, 1994)

Personnel:
Morrissey: vocals
Siouxsie Sioux: vocals
Produced by Boz Boorer

'Interlude' (George De La Rue/Hal Shaper)

This one-off collaboration with Siouxsie Sioux (of Siouxsie & The Banshees), released on August 8th 1994 has often been seen as evidence that Morrissey is difficult to work with, as there have been quite a lot of rumours about how poorly the pair got on during the recording. For example, it's suggested that that Morrissey only communicated with Siouxsie via fax. But despite all this, it's a great single, which eventually peaked at a disappointing #25 in the UK. The song was suggested by Morrissey, and they both recorded the whole song separately before Boorer (who produced the session) mixed the two recordings into a duet. The string section came from Britpop band, My Life Story, which formed the year before, in 1993, and their contribution made it sound quite similar to Timi Yuro's original recording from 1968, which was made for the movie of the same name. Allegedly, Morrissey fell out with Siouxsie while discussing the music video that was planned to promote the single, and it meant that the release was delayed for a year. Morrissey's solo recording of the song was eventually released on the *Very Best of Morrissey* compilation in 2011. The cover photo of Eileen Sheekey was taken by Roger Mayne.

The extended version on the single's B-side is just a longer mix of the song made by Boorer. The other B-side, on the 12' single and the CD single, was an instrumental version.

Boxers (EP, 1995)

Personnel:
Morrissey: vocals
Alain Whyte: guitars
Boz Boorer: guitars, clarinet, saxophone
Jonny Bridgwood: bass guitar
Woodie Taylor: drums

'Boxers' (Morrissey/Whyte)

In February 1995, Morrissey was about to tour the UK for the first time in a couple of years and to have some new songs to play, he released this EP on January 16 (it peaked at #23 in the UK). The title track reflected his love of boxing, something that would be even more clear on his next album, *Southpaw Grammar*, and is a beautiful pop song – a prime example of Alain Whyte at his very best. The lyrics, about a boxer who's losing in his hometown (but the crowd loves him anyway), are great as well, and this was a great way for Morrissey to keep up the momentum from the popular *Vauxhall and I* album. The sampled voice of the commentator in the song belongs to BBC's Reg Gutteridge. A music video was also made for the song, where Cornelius Carr fights a boxer named Sunny (a still from the video was used for the cover of the 'World of Morrissey' compilation later in 1995), which might be a reference to the song with the same name that was supposed to be included on the EP but was later released on its own.

'Have-a-Go Merchant' (Morrissey/Whyte)

In 1993, Natalie Merchant and her band, 10 000 Maniacs, recorded a cover of 'Everyday Is Like Sunday' for their single 'Candy Everybody Wants'. So, did this trigger Morrissey to write this song about her? It's not really known, but it's a nice pop song. With it's surprising pub-sing-along chorus, it sounds rather like it's about a drunk man who's neglecting his daughter while he's out picking a fight with everyone he meets. In all fairness, it's probably a play on words, and even though it might be a reference to Natalie, the title works on its own anyway.

'Whatever Happens, I Love You' (Morrissey/Whyte)

This was probably the first time that I really noticed Boorer playing clarinet on a Morrissey recording, and it's really hard to miss it in this song, as it almost sounds like an alarm at times. The lyrics, about a crashed relationship, are classic Morrissey, and even though the song might not be his most beloved, I have liked it since I first heard it back in 1995. It was also picked to be the opening track on the compilation *World of Morrissey* that came out later that same year, which might indicate that the song meant something to Moz.

World of Morrissey (compilation, 1995)

Personnel:
Morrissey: vocals, sleeve design
Alain Whyte: guitars, backing vocals
Boz Boorer: guitars, clarinet, saxophone
Jonny Bridgewood: bass guitar
Gary Day: bass guitar
Woodie Taylor: drums
Spencer James Cobrin: drums
Chrissie Hynde: backing vocals on 'My Love Life'
James O'Brien: photography (of Cornelius Carr)
Produced by Steve Lillywhite, Clive Langer, Alan Winstanley, Stephen Street and Mark Ronson
Playing time: 54:54
Label: Parlophone (UK)
Release date: February 6 1995
Highest chart position: UK: 15

At the time, most fans and critics didn't really see the point of this compilation, released the year after Morrissey's big comeback with the successful album *Vauxhall and I*. It's made up of some singles, some B-sides, some live tracks and some album tracks, in no particular order, and at first glance, it seems obvious to agree with the critics. But despite all this, it's undoubtedly a collection of fine songs, even if the selection might be a bit haphazard. For instance, where are the other singles, like 'Pregnant for the Last Time' and 'Interlude'? Maybe he didn't like them anymore. That wouldn't surprise me when it comes to Moz.

The title of the compilation is a tribute to a series of compilations released by Decca in the 60s and 70s to promote their current stars, many of them old favourites of Morrissey's (like Billy Fury). The sleeve was not made to resemble these at all, though, and instead sports a photo of boxer Cornelius Carr (taken from the music video for the song 'Boxers').

Released during the Britpop peak in the UK, the album might have performed brilliantly but failed to live up to its expectations and didn't even crack the top ten in the UK. In 2010, the compilation was deleted from the EMI (Parlophone) catalogue, together with the live album *Beethoven Was Deaf* (1993), and the later compilation *Suedehead: The Best of Morrissey* (1997), making them unavailable in the record shops. The latter two are still available on the streaming sites, though.

'Whatever Happens, I Love You' (Morrissey/Whyte)

(see *Boxers EP*)

'Billy Budd' (Morrissey/Whyte)

(see *Vauxhall and I* album)

'Jack the Ripper' (Morrissey/Boorer)

This song, which was the first that Morrissey wrote with Boz Boorer, was originally recorded in the studio in October 1992 at the last *Your Arsenal* session with producer Mick Ronson. None of the people involved with the recording were happy with the way it turned out, but despite this it was released as the B-side of the 'Certain People I Know' single in 1992. The song was also played live for many years, and the version on this compilation was recorded at the Paris Zenith on December 22nd 1992, and then released on the live album *Beethoven Was Deaf*, which came out in 1993. The live recording is actually a bit better than the studio version, and it comes as no surprise that it's about the London serial killer known by the same name, though the lyrics aren't very detailed. Sadly, the live version omits the outro from the studio version, with Morrissey chanting 'nobody knows me', which adds a certain air to the song. But Boorer's tune is harrowing enough in itself if you ask me.

'Have-a-Go Merchant' (Morrissey/Whyte)

(see *Boxers* EP)

'The Loop' (Morrissey/Nevin)

Another one of the rockabilly songs that Morrissey and his band recorded during the *Kill Uncle* sessions in 1991, and this is more or less instrumental, with just some brief lyrics (where Morrissey sends a message to a friend to 'by all means, call me'). According to songwriter Mark Nevin, he gave the song its title on the demo cassette he gave to Morrissey, and they then decided to keep it for the finished song. When played live by his new rockabilly-style band, the track was sped up quite a bit, which can be heard on the *Beethoven Was Deaf* live album.

'Sister I'm a Poet' (Morrissey/Street)

Originally released as a B-side of the 'Everyday Is Like Sunday' single in 1988, this live version was recorded at the Paris Zenith on December 22 1992, and released on *Beethoven Was Deaf*. This live rendition was adapted to the rockabilly phase Morrissey was going through in 1991-1992, turning the original Smiths-like arrangement into a foot-tapping 50s rock tune instead, which suits it very well. In the lyrics, Moz recalls his youth in Manchester, where he was the weird, bohemian poet.

'You're the One for Me, Fatty' (Morrissey/Whyte)

Another live version, this one recorded in London on December 20 1992, and released on *Beethoven Was Deaf*. The original song is on the *Your Arsenal* album, and this recording sounds more or less the same as the studio version, as it's the same backing band and was released the same year.

'Boxers' (Morrissey/Whyte)

(see *Boxers* EP)

'Moonriver' (Henry Mancini/Johnny Mercer)
Something of a crooner standard for the past 60 years (especially for Andy Williams, who recorded it in 1962), the song was written for the movie *Breakfast at Tiffany's* (1961), where it was performed by actor Audrey Hepburn. Morrissey recorded his version (where he decided to condense the original two-word title into one word, 'Moonriver') for the 'Hold On to Your Friends' single in 1995, mainly with just guitar and omnichord. For the 12' single, he recorded an 'extended version' of the song, clocking in at ten minutes, and the cries of actor Peggy Evans (from the movie *The Blue Lamp*, 1950) can be heard in the background. It's the 12' version that can be heard on this compilation.

'My Love Life' (Morrissey/Nevin)
(see 'My Love Life' single)

'Certain People I Know' (Morrissey/Whyte)
(see *Your Arsenal* album)

'The Last of the Famous International Playboys' (Morrissey/Street)
(see 'The Last of the Famous International Playboys' single)

'We'll Let You Know' (Morrissey/Whyte)
(see *Your Arsenal* album)

'Spring-Heeled Jim' (Morrissey/Boorer)
(see *Vauxhall and I* album)

Southpaw Grammar (album, 1995)

Personnel:
Morrissey: vocals
Boz Boorer: guitars
Alain Whyte: guitars
Jonny Bridgwood: bass guitar
Spencer James Cobrin: drums
Rankin: photography
Recorded at Hook End Manor
Produced by Steve Lillywhite
Playing time: 47:50
Label: RCA Victor (UK), Reprise (US)
Release date: August 28 1995
Highest chart position: UK: 4, US: 66

After the roaring success of *Vauxhall and I*, the pressure was on for Morrissey, as he had finally arrived back in the big league in the UK, both commercially and critically. The non-album EP *Boxers,* which came out in early 1995, kept on walking on the same path, with melodic, guitar-based pop songs, but for the album, Morrissey decided that he needed a change instead of recording '*Vauxhall and I* 2.0'.

First of all, he left EMI and Parlophone for a deal with another major label, RCA, and he somehow convinced them to bring their original name, RCA Victor, back to life. It was the full name of the label from its formation in 1929 until the mid-1970s, when the Victor part was dropped from the record labels and sleeves. This would actually be the first in a long run of new labels for Morrissey, as he left RCA after this album and ended up on Island Records for his next record (*Maladjusted*).

Secondly, he decided to stick with his band from the previous album, and also ended up with Steve Lillywhite as producer again (he asked both Brian Eno and Chris Thomas but they turned him down). Lillywhite booked the Miraval studio in Provence, France, for recording the new album, but since Morrissey didn't like the rundown old manor, he returned home after just one night, leaving the band on their own to record some backing tracks. Sadly, the songs tracked there were later scrapped, as they were recorded in the wrong key (as Morrissey's tape recorder had played the demo cassettes that Alain Whyte and Boz Boorer gave him at the wrong speed), so they had to go at it again.

For the second recording session, Morrissey and the band were back at Hook End Manor, after touring the UK in early February. By now Woodie Taylor had left the band, and was replaced by Spencer Cobrin, who had played on *Your Arsenal.* The main reason for this was probably that Cobrin was a more rock-oriented drummer than Taylor, and Morrissey had a clear idea that he wanted to go in that very direction on the record.

Many fans were puzzled by the album at the time of its release, and as Britpop was at its height at this time (many Britpop bands were very influenced by The Smiths), it was surprising that their biggest influence would record quite an experimental rock album instead of a pop masterpiece. And it is indeed an unusual Morrissey album – it's just eight songs long, but also his longest solo record, with two of the songs being more than ten minutes long. The long instrumental parts are also a rare thing in the Moz discography, with both lengthy guitar interludes and extended drum solos.

So, despite the success of the previous album, *Southpaw Grammar* failed to live up to expectations, both commercially (it peaked at #4 in the UK, but didn't last very long in the charts) and critically, as the critics were as puzzled as the fans. None of the two singles released from the album ('Dagenham Dave' and 'The Boy Racer') made it to the top twenty in the UK singles chart either.

The album was remastered and re-released in 2009, and once again, Morrissey decided to 'mess up' the running order and add some more songs to the tracklist – 'Nobody Loves Us' (B-side to 'Dagenham Dave'), 'Honey, You Know Where To Find Me' (studio outtake from the album sessions), 'You Should Have Been Nice To Me' (studio outtake from the album sessions), and 'Fantastic Bird' (studio outtake from *Your Arsenal*). The album also got a new sleeve design, replacing the original photo of a boxer with a black and white photo of Morrissey, taken by Linder Sterling.

'The Teachers Are Afraid of the Pupils' (Morrissey/Boorer)

This Boorer composition is notable for being the longest song Morrissey has ever recorded, with its eleven minutes and fifteen seconds (reportedly, Morrissey wanted the song to be exactly that long), and also for containing a sample from a classical piece (Dmitri Shostakovich's *Fifth Symphony in D Minor* from 1937). The lyrics mark a return to the school world for Morrissey, and you could say that after taking the side of the pupils in 'The Headmaster Ritual' (on *Meat Is Murder*), he was now taking the teachers' side, as they had to battle threatful pupils and parents. At the end of the song, you can hear a sample from the 1954 movie *Eight O'clock Walk*, which has a schoolboy reciting a poem.

'Reader Meet Author' (Morrissey/Boorer)

After the experimental opening track, we're back in old familiar Morrissey land, with this quite straightforward pop song about authors and journalists who act as if they are more working-class than they really are. Morrissey has later said that this is his favourite song off the album and that it's the best song he has ever written with Boorer – which might be a stretch – but it's nonetheless a good song and something of a blueprint of what Morrissey would sound like for the next couple of decades.

'The Boy Racer' (Morrissey/Whyte)

Released as the second single (and Morrissey's twentieth solo single) off the album on November 27 1995 (peaking at #36 in the UK), this takes us back to the rockier sound of *Your Arsenal*, and we're also back to the character songs. This one is about a speeding youngster with plenty of money and women in his life, which is something that the singer is both annoyed by and envious of ('He's just too good-natured and / He's got too much money and / He's got too many girlfriends / I'm jealous, that's all'). A bit rockier than the first single ('Dagenham Dave'), it didn't make a big impression on the record buyers, who had got used to fabulous B-sides all through Morrissey's career, and now all they got was a couple of live recordings (Smiths song 'London', and three songs from *Vauxhall and I*). To make an even more obvious point of the song's heavy sound, Morrissey and the band (except for Bridgwood) are surrounded by Marshall stacks in the music video, in which Morrissey is also pulled over by cops and gets frisked against the police car.

'The Operation' (Morrissey/Whyte)

Extended drum solos aren't something that you would normally associate with Morrissey, but here you are treated to one that lasts more than two minutes, courtesy of Spencer Cobrin. When the song was played live, the solo was always omitted, which might have been a wise decision (but Morrissey did use the drum intro as entrance music during his tours in 1997 and 1999). When the song ends, you have basically spent the last seven minutes listening to drums and guitars, interjected by some vocals about a former friend who has changed for the worse. I think most people tended to skip this song when listening to the album.

'Dagenham Dave' (Morrissey/Whyte)

This was the first single, released on August 21 1995, just a week before the album came out, peaking at #26 in the UK. The chart performance was of course a disappointment for Morrissey, but as the Britpop wave hit the UK full scale, this new Moz sound seemed terribly out of date (the *NME* said that 'Morrissey has become the embarrassing incontinent grandfather of britpop' in their review). As you can see from its title, it's yet another character song, this time about a rather unpleasant boy who eats a lot of pie and has his head down women's blouses. Musically, it's a bit like a mix of old Morrissey and new Morrissey, or a heavy pop song, if you like. Oh, and it's got nothing to do with the Stranglers song with the same name.

'Do Your Best and Don't Worry' (Morrissey/Whyte)

Recorded just before the album was mixed, this song is the only one on the album where bass player Bridgwood isn't playing. Instead, Boz Boorer handled the bass here, and it's yet another rocker, more reminiscent of *Your Arsenal* than *Vauxhall and I*. It's not hard to imagine that Morrissey wrote the lyrics as a pep talk to himself while recording the album, but he was reportedly very happy with the finished song. The highlight of the song is the coda, where Whyte adds some high-pitched backing vocals through the guitar pick up (this effect can be heard on many songs on the album) and Cobrin's drums sound like a machine gun.

'Best Friend on the Payroll' (Morrissey/Whyte)

Hardly anyone's favourite, it's often alleged that the lyrics are about Jake Walters, a photographer who acted as Morrissey's bodyguard and personal assistant, and who also lived with him in his Camden apartment a few years earlier (Walters took many of the photos used for the singles released from *Vauxhall and I*, and there has been speculation about the two having a romantic relationship at some point). Basically, what he's trying to get across here is that you should never have business relationships with your friends, which is probably good advice. Musically, it's not much to tell the grandchildren about really – a basic, poppy rock song in the standard new Morrissey style.

'Southpaw' (Morrissey/Whyte)

This is as close as we get to a title track on this album, and it's also the second song on the album lasting more than ten minutes! It all kicks off with chaotic guitar noise, eventually turning into a five-minute-long rock song with a mish-mash of flashbacks from his youth (with lines that could easily be interpreted as being about Morrissey's relationship to his own mother), and thoughts about lost friendships. Then after five minutes, Morrissey steps back and lets the band go on for another five minutes, with the guitars chugging along to Cobrin's steady beat, bringing it all to a sudden halt at exactly ten minutes– according to Bridgwood, the tape ended. This is a really odd piece in the Moz discography, and a lot of fans probably wondered what he was on about. But at the same time, you have to admire his guts in going for it.

'Honey, You Know Where to Find Me' (Morrissey/Boorer)

Recorded during the album sessions, this song had to wait until 2009 to see the light of day, at least officially, as it was included on the remastered and extended reissue (it was also released on 10' vinyl for Record Store Day 2020). The lyrics to the song were originally written for a totally different tune written by Alain Whyte for *Vauxhall and I*, but Morrissey then decided to scrap that song and instead use the words for this Boorer composition. Listening to it now, it's hard to ignore the feeling that it still sounds like an outtake, and it's a bit of a mystery why Morrissey put it on the revamped album. In the sleeve notes to the reissue, Morrissey revealed that the place that he could be found was the pub The Good Mixer in Camden, where he lived at the time.

'Fantastic Bird' (Morrissey/Whyte)
For some weird reason, Morrissey decided to take this *Your Arsenal* outtake, recorded in 1992, and release it on the 2009 reissue of *Southpaw Grammar* (and also on the aforementioned Record Store Day 10' single in 2020). Musically, it sounds like most of the *Your Arsenal* material, and so did some of this album, so maybe it made more sense than it appeared to. It was originally recorded as a B-side to the 'Certain People I Know' single, but then it was scrapped, and I would guess that the band thought it would never emerge again. The lyrics are weird, to say the least, and the 'bird' in the title is not the flying one with feathers. No, it would appear to be about a 'metal bird' (which could be interpreted as a rocket ship), with the person in the song wanting to be the first stand-up comedian in outer space. Did I mention that it was weird?

'You Should Have Been Nice to Me' (Morrissey/Boorer)
Another outtake recorded during the album sessions, and this one was mostly recorded at the Miraval studio when Morrissey went home and left the band to their own devices. Musically, it sounds more like a *Vauxhall and I* song, with its acoustic guitars and soft arrangement, and lyrically it's like a sibling to 'Hold on to Your Friends', as it deals mainly with friends who suddenly aren't there for you. It's far from Morrissey's prime material, and as it doesn't really suit the rest of the album, it was probably a good decision to omit it from the original release. This was the third and final track on the Record Store Day 10' single in 2020.

'Nobody Loves Us' (Morrissey/Whyte)
This is the only song among the extra tracks on the reissue that was previously released, as the B-side on the 'Dagenham Dave' single. As opposed to the previous song, this one would actually have been a great choice for inclusion on the original album release, and Morrissey told US radio station KCXX Radio San Bernadino in August 1998 that this was one of his favourites among his songs. It was also one of the songs recorded as an instrumental at Miraval, but it was later re-recorded with Cobrin on drums, and that was the version that was eventually released. As you might guess from the title, this is one of many Moz lyrics putting the outsiders, born-again atheists and practicing troublemakers in the limelight.

Contemporary Singles

Sunny (single, 1995)
Personnel:
Morrissey: vocals
Alain Whyte: guitars
Boz Boorer: guitars
Jonny Bridgwood: bass guitar
Woodie Taylor: drums

'Sunny' (Morrissey/Whyte)

This lovely, jangly, poppy Whyte tune was originally intended as the fourth song on the *Boxers* EP, which was released earlier in 1995. But luckily, Morrissey felt that the song was good enough to release on its own on December 11, which was a good call. However, since it was released on Parlophone just a few weeks after 'The Boy Racer' came out on another label (RCA Victor), the promotion was minimal, and it stalled in the UK charts just below the top 40 (peaking at #42). In the lyrics, Moz tells the story of a friend who was lost to drug abuse, making it one of many songs about this subject in his solo catalogue. A music video, made later for inclusion as a multimedia track on the US only rarities compilation *My Early Burglary Years* (1998), was directed by James O'Brien.

'Black-Eyed Susan' (Morrissey/Whyte)

Originally written for the *Vauxhall and I* album, the song was then a far rockier affair, sounding like a *Your Arsenal* outtake. But then suddenly Morrissey had one of his trademark changes of mind and wanted to rearrange the whole song. It was made into a pop song, and he also scrapped the middle verse, instead asking his band to just play something weird in its place, which explains the very odd experimental and instrumental section in the middle of the track. The recording was then put on the scrapheap until it turned up on this B-side two years later. And despite the song sharing its name with a famous 19th-century play, that's about the only thing the two have in common, as Morrissey instead sings about a lazy friend called Susan.

'A Swallow on My Neck' (Morrissey/Whyte)

This lovely pop tune was recorded in 1994, at the same time as 'Moonriver', and was originally planned as a B-side of 'Hold on to Your Friends' or 'The More You Ignore Me, the Closer I Get'. Morrissey said in an interview with US radio station KCXX in August 1998, that the song was about getting a tattoo on your neck, which he thought was an impressive sight (there is also a tattoo of a swallow on the hands on the back cover of *Vauxhall and I*).

Maladjusted (1997)

Personnel:
Morrissey: vocals
Boz Boorer: guitars, clarinet
Alain Whyte: guitars, piano, backing vocals
Jonny Bridgwood: bass guitar
Spencer Cobrin: drums
Rankin: photography
Recorded at Hook End Manor
Produced by Steve Lillywhite
Playing time: 42:54
Label: Mercury/Island (UK), Mercury (US)
Release date: August 11 1997
Highest chart position: UK: 8

Two years after the release of *Southpaw Grammar*, almost to the day, Morrissey's sixth studio album was released, and during the time that had passed since we last heard from him, he had mostly been dealing with the Mike Joyce trial – which is quite obvious when listening to this record.

So, the trial, then. It all dates back to The Smiths days, as Andy Rourke and Mike Joyce discovered that the contract that the band signed with Rough Trade had only been signed by Morrissey and Johnny Marr, which meant that according to the contract, The Smiths was just Morrissey and Marr, with two additional musicians. This also meant that the royalties for record sales etc., were mostly given to the two songwriters. When Rourke and Joyce discovered this, they pressed charges against their two former bandmates in order to get the royalties they thought they deserved. In the end, Rourke settled out of court, but Joyce wanted to take it further, and the trial took place in High Court in December 1996, where Morrissey and Marr lost the case– the judge John Weeks famously called Morrissey 'devious, truculent and unreliable' during the trial.

A few weeks after the trial ended, Morrissey was back in his favourite studio, Hook End Manor, with the same band as he had used for the previous album, and with a bunch of new songs to record, for an album originally titled 'Ambitious Outsiders'. Since *Your Arsenal*, Whyte and Boorer had been writing more or less 50 per cent each of the songs on the albums, but now drummer Cobrin threw himself into the fight and contributed the song 'Wide to Receive' to this new album (he also wrote two songs that ended up on single B-sides – 'Now I Am a Was' and 'Lost'), while Whyte eventually got seven songs on the record, and Boorer three.

Maladjusted did get a rather lukewarm reception when it was released, both by music critics and most fans, and I would guess Morrissey wasn't too pleased with either in hindsight, as he gave it a real makeover when it was re-released in 2009, together with Southpaw Grammar'. In this case, he removed two songs ('Papa Jack' and 'Roy's Keen') and added six songs originally released on the three singles that were associated with the album ('Lost', 'Heir Apparent', 'The Edges Are No Longer Parallel', 'This Is Not Your Country', 'Now I Am a Was', and 'I Can Have Both'), plus 'Sorrow Will Come In The End' finally got an official UK release. He also took the opportunity to replace the quite horrible original artwork with a much better photo of himself, taken near King's Cross in London.

'Maladjusted' (Morrissey/Boorer)

So, we kick off with the title track, which in turn kicks off with feedback guitars and then a sample of actor Anthony Newley saying: 'on this glorious occasion, of the splendid defeat,' taken from the movie *The Cockleshell Heroes* (José Ferrer, 1955). What follows is more or less an almost five-minute-long verse without a proper chorus (the demo consisted of more parts, but Morrissey only liked one of them, so they decided to go with just that one), where Morrissey wants to 'start from before the beginning' and goes on to tell a somewhat unfocused story about restless youth walking around in London stealing wine and peeping into people's houses. Although the song may lack a proper chorus, that doesn't make it a less powerful song, and considering the rest of the album, this is probably one of the best tracks on it.

'Alma Matters' (Morrissey/Whyte)

Morrissey was back in the UK top 20 with the release of this single (peaking at #16) in July 1997, just a week before the album came out. This is a rather typical Whyte song, which means that it's a bit more poppy than Boorer's tunes, and that makes it a bit unexpected that it's also the longest song on the album with its four minutes and 48 seconds. Quite a change from the previous album, right? When asked to explain the meaning of the lyrics, Morrissey said that he wanted to say that we should be proud of the female side of ourselves, or the male side if you're female, and that it doesn't matter how you behave. He later backed away from this statement, but I think there might be some truth to it anyway. This song also marked a return to Morrissey's old favourite *A Taste of Honey* by Shelagh Delaney, which he borrowed from quite a bit in his Smiths days. Here, it's the line 'It's your life, ruin it your own way' that Moz adapted for his lyrics. And yes, the title is a play on 'Alma mater', which is a Latin term used for naming your old school.

'Ambitious Outsiders' (Morrissey/Whyte)

When it wasn't used as the album title, Morrissey wrote a song with the same name instead, and it's a really disturbing one, too. He's not known for shying away from controversial subjects, but I think he really outdid himself here, when we wrote a song written from the point of view of a gang of paedophiles, and even hints at blaming the parents for having kids in the first place in the last lines of the lyrics. Quite surprisingly, the song didn't cause a stir when the album was released (maybe everyone was focusing on the Mike Joyce bashing on 'Sorrow Will Come in The End'). Musically, Morrissey and the band try to give the horrible and dark lyrics some appropriate backing, but sadly they (and producer Lillywhite) opted for synth strings instead of the real deal, which makes it all sound like a half-baked idea, really.

'Trouble Loves Me' (Morrissey/Whyte)
The song title is classic Morrissey in itself, and the song isn't bad either! What first sounds like a pure piano ballad soon turns into a full-band affair, but Whyte's piano is undoubtedly the lead character here, as Morrissey once again turns towards self-pity. And while longing for true love, as always, he also expresses a longing for danger, or trouble if you prefer, apparent in the first lines of the song ('Trouble loves me / Trouble needs me / Two things more than you do'). Most fans seem to agree that this is the highlight of this album, and it may appear that Morrissey thinks so too, as this is the only song from the album that has been played live in recent years.

'Papa Jack' (Morrissey/Whyte)
If the previous song was the fan favourite of the album, this could easily be described as the opposite (along with 'Roy's Keen'), where Morrissey is possibly using the Papa as a metaphor for a former pop star who regrets his behaviour in the past. The song starts off with just Whyte's guitar as accompaniment, but it soon changes and turns into yet another bombastic rock track. Of its four and a half minute running time, Morrissey is singing on two and a half, leaving Whyte to act like a rock star for the remaining two minutes. This song was omitted when the album was reissued, remastered and rearranged in 2009, and I think most people can understand why.

'Ammunition' (Morrissey/Boorer)
This song is a good example of how the arrangement and production of a song can lift it to brilliant heights or make it sink to the bottom. Well, maybe sinking to the bottom is a bit too harsh here, but if this song would have been treated like the songs on *Vauxhall and I,* it could have been a lot better. The lyrics, about not needing revenge, weren't really true for Morrissey (see 'Sorrow Will Come in the End'), but that didn't stop him from considering releasing the song as a single.

'Wide To Receive' (Morrissey/Cobrin)
After three albums with songs by just Whyte and Boorer (except for two by Mark Nevin on *Your Arsenal*), drummer Spencer Cobrin suddenly entered the scene as a songwriter, contributing this Whyte-esque ballad, which Morrissey said was supposed to be an 'internet song'. This might sound a bit cryptic, but he apparently imagined someone lying by their computer waiting for someone to 'tap into you and finding that nobody is'. Did that make it less cryptic? The

song was originally recorded as a B-side, but in the last second, Morrissey decided to swap it for 'I Can Have Both' which was added to the album in 2009.

'Roy's Keen' (Morrissey/Whyte)

This is probably one of the least liked songs in the entire Morrissey catalogue, and it's mostly down to the lyrics, which show the singer at his silliest, and bleakest. In general, his attempts at humour often aren't very well received, and for good reason. Morrissey still thought it was a good idea to release it as the second single off the album, but it didn't even make it to the UK top 40 (peaking at #42). The bad chart performance also resulted in the shelving of a recording the band did for BBC's *Top of the Pops*, though it would be shown later in the archive show, *Top of the Pops 2*, in 2003. The title of this song is, obviously, a pun on Roy Keane, an Irish footballer who used to play for Manchester United, but this Roy is a window cleaner who really loves his work. Musically, it's not that bad – more or less an ordinary Whyte pop song – but that didn't really help this time. In an interview with Paul Nolan of Hot Press in 2008, Morrissey said that he had no idea what he was thinking when he wrote this song. Well, you and me both, Moz. The song was, not surprisingly, removed for the 2009 reissue.

'He Cried' (Morrissey/Whyte)

Another mid-tempo Whyte song, with the usual suspects when it comes to melody and chords – it's one of those songs that you can almost sing along to the first time you hear it. The crying man in the lyrics could be Morrissey himself, singing about tears of sadness from not being needed or wanted, but he has never confirmed this in any way. It's not anyone's favourite song on the album, but hardly anyone's choice for the worst one either.

'Sorrow Will Come in the End' (Morrissey/Whyte)

Well, it's actually hard to find the right words when describing this 'song'. It was omitted from the original UK release of the album, as the label feared a lawsuit, for good reason. In this spoken-word piece, Morrissey attacks Mike Joyce and everyone involved in the court case that he and Marr lost the previous year, and he's not being particularly shy about it, either (the 'chorus' just contains the words 'Lawyer! Liar!'). The musical backing to this rant is at times almost hilarious in its contrast to the words Morrissey is uttering, especially in the 'don't close your eyes' part, with its circus-like melody. One could imagine that Morrissey's wounds might have healed when he prepared the 2009 reissue of the album, as he had a chance to remove it once and for all, but no. Instead, the track got its first official UK release. On the following tour in 1997, Morrissey said 'this next song is called 'Sorrow Will Come in The End'', and instead played 'Shoplifters of the World Unite'. I think we were all very happy that he did.

'Satan Rejected My Soul' (Morrissey/Boorer)
A classic Morrissey title (I remember buying a t-shirt with the title on its back at Morrissey's first-ever concert in Sweden, during the *Maladjusted* tour) and classic Morrissey tune. Released as the final single off the album on December 29th 1997, it barely made it to the UK top 40 (peaking at #39), and therefore didn't succeed in bringing him back to the big league, which was what the label had hoped for – as this was classic Moz. Musically, it brings back the glam influences from *Your Arsenal*, but even though the riff is notable throughout the song, it doesn't really take centre stage. In the lyrics, Morrissey reconnects with his song, 'There's a Place in Hell for Me and My Friends', in a way, as he now seems to realise that even the devil doesn't want him, after all ('as low as he goes, he never quite goes this low'). When released as a single, this would be the last Morrissey release of the century, and also the last song on the original release of the album. And it was quite a fitting one, as well.

'Lost' (Morrissey/Cobrin)
Originally released as the B-side to the unsuccessful 'Roy's Keen' single, this Cobrin song found its way back to the limelight when it was included on the re-released version of the album in 2009. The song was described by Simon Goddard in *Mozipedia* as a 'fitting metaphor for the relationship between Morrissey and his audience', and sure enough, the fans took this one to their hearts – I suppose they felt that they were as lost in this world as their idol. Cobrin's slow tune was really nothing special, but that didn't stop Morrissey from naming this his favourite among his drummer's songs, although that doesn't say that much, really.

'Heir Apparent' (Morrissey/Whyte)
This catchy Whyte song would actually have been a good choice for inclusion on the original album, but instead, Morrissey decided to stick it in on the B-side to the first single off the album, 'Alma Matters' (presumably, he later realised his mistake, as it was included on the album redux in 2009). In the lyrics, he returns to his beloved/hated Manchester and sees a younger version of himself wanting to make the same journey that he did more than a decade ago, while he tries his best to change his younger self's mind. This is actually like 'London' in reverse once again, though Moz is not really sure the trip to London is worth it at this point…

'The Edges Are No Longer Parallel' (Morrissey/Whyte)
Another B-side to 'Roy's Keen' (available on the 12' and CD versions of the single), this is often mentioned when listing Morrissey's best solo songs, which makes it quite a mystery as to why he decided to keep it off the original album. The song title is supposed to be a metaphor for a relationship that has gone from being meaningful to being meaningless, and Morrissey ends the song by exclaiming that his only mistake was to 'hope'. And speaking of the end,

the song goes from being a soft, acoustic song to an explosion of guitars and drums. This is allegedly one of Whyte's favourites among the songs he wrote for Morrissey, and it's not hard to see why.

'This Is Not Your Country' (Morrissey/Whyte)

Apart from the two lengthy songs on the *Southpaw Grammar* album, Morrissey isn't normally one to release songs that stretch beyond the five-minute mark, but here's one that ends after almost seven and a half minutes, taken from the B-side of the 'Satan Rejected My Soul' single (the 12' and CD versions). The title of the song probably made many Moz fans a bit uncomfortable, with the racism debate from 'National Front Disco' in mind, but this wasn't actually a song with a racist theme. Instead, it focuses on the conflict in Northern Ireland, and the BBC coverage of it in particular, with Morrissey going as far as to call the broadcasting corporation 'scum'. Musically, it's an attempt at creating something of an epic, political ballad, but those synth strings more or less mess it up.

'I Can Have Both' (Morrissey/Boorer)

This jangly tune was originally intended to be included on the album, but at the last minute, Morrissey changed his mind and omitted it in favour of 'Wide To Receive' (which allegedly upset Boorer at the time). This is a bit of a mystery to me, as this lovely pop song would have been one of the highlights of the album, so it's wonderful that it was included in 2009. The lyrics are widely believed to be something of a 'coming out' for Morrissey as bisexual, in which he's happy that he can make a choice of his own nowadays, as opposed to when he was a 'small shy boy'. In the sleeve notes to the 2009 reissue of the album, Morrissey says this is one of his favourite songs. Have we heard that before?

'Now I Am a Was' (Morrissey/Cobrin)

The third and final Cobrin song on the redux version of the album, the title could easily be interpreted as Morrissey reflecting on his status as a former pop star who now barely reached the upper parts of the charts. But as tempting as that may be, it's probably more correct to read it as a reflection of a crashed relationship. The song, which again sounds a lot like a standard Whyte tune, was included on the 'Satan Rejected My Soul' single, which would be Morrissey's last release until he returned to the scene in 2004 with the now classic 'Irish Blood, English Heart'.

You Are the Quarry (album, 2004)

Personnel:
Morrissey: vocals, sleeve design
Boz Boorer: guitars
Alain Whyte: guitars, backing vocals
Gary Day: bass guitar
Dean Butterworth: drums
Roger Manning: keyboards
Greg Gorman: photography
Recorded at Hook End Manor (UK) and Conway (US)
Produced by Jerry Finn
Playing time: 47:20
Label: Sanctuary/Attack (UK)
Release date: May 17 2004
Highest chart position: UK: 2, US: 11

Following the somewhat disappointing experience of *Maladjusted*, Morrissey was dropped by Island Records and was then without a label for almost seven years. Many fans probably thought that this was it for the former pop star. There were not a lot of signs of life in form of new music from old Mozzer (the releases that came out were just a few compilations – for instance, the US only 'rarities' collection *My Early Burglary Years*, and the singles box sets *The CD Singles 88-91 / The CD Singles 91-95*), but he did go on two world tours, one in 1999/2000, and one in 2002, with no albums to promote, and no label backing him up.

After the release of *Maladjusted*, Morrissey decided to leave the UK for good and moved to Los Angeles, where he would reside for many years. While most people forgot about him at the end of the century, he bided his time with writing songs, and then when he decided it was time to make a comeback to the music scene, he did it with impeccable timing. In 2002, The Smiths were voted the most important band in pop history by *NME*, and at the same time, he went on a very successful UK tour. On his earlier tours (apart from the one following *Maladjusted*), he refused to play Smiths songs, but now he changed his mind, which delighted his fans.

After months of rumour, Morrissey announced in May 2003 that he had finally signed a deal with Sanctuary Records. Feeling that the name of the label wasn't very fitting for him, Sanctuary decided to revive the old reggae/ska label Attack (which was originally operating during the 70s) for him, much like RCA did with their Victor sublabel back in 1995 for *Southpaw Grammar*. With a deal finally in hand, Morrissey brought his backing band from the recent tour to his old favourite studio, Hook End Manor, to record what would be his seventh studio album. Whyte and Boorer were still handling the guitars, Gary Day was enlisted on bass again (for the first time since *Your Arsenal*), and Dean Butterworth played the drums. He also hired Roger Joseph Manning Jr (of Jellyfish) as keyboardist. The producer's chair was occupied by Jerry Finn, which was a somewhat surprising choice, as he was mostly known for working with bands like Bad Religion and Green Day, but then again... isn't making surprising decisions something that is quite typical of Morrissey?

The album was originally going to be called 'Irish Blood, English Heart', but a few months before the release in May 2004, the correct title was announced: *You Are the Quarry*. On the cover, Moz is posing with a machine gun, looking like an Al Capone gangster (in some countries, the sleeve photo was cropped to omit the gun from the cover art), which can be seen as both a reference to the title and the name of the label.

Both critics and fans were delighted, and many saw it as a smashing comeback album, climbing to number two on the UK album chart, his biggest success since *Vauxhall And I* a decade earlier. The singles were equally successful, which made him the only artist to have four UK top ten hits in a row in 2004.

A few months after the original release, the album was released in a new edition (which was the new trend in the record industry), with a bonus disc containing the B-sides to the first three singles taken from the album and a few videos.

'America Is Not the World' (Morrissey/Whyte)

Even though Morrissey had fled the UK to buy a house in Los Angeles, he still thought it would be a good idea to write a song about what was wrong with his new home country, like the current president (George W Bush) and the US influence on the rest of the world. While Morrissey was brave enough to make this very political song the opening song on his comeback album, the music sounded like a studio outtake from *Maladjusted* or *Southpaw Grammar*, which means that this was yet another typical Whyte tune.

'Irish Blood, English Heart' (Morrissey/Whyte)

What would originally have been the album title track (released in early May 2004 around the world) instead became the comeback single. And what a comeback it was! It peaked at #3 in the UK (which is his highest-charting single ever there, along with 'You Have Killed Me'), and it also peaked at #4 in Sweden, #7 in Canada, and #17 in Ireland and Belgium. It's hard to deny the power of this song. It was actually recorded way before Morrissey did his version, as Whyte wrote it for his band, Johnny Panic and the Bible of Dreams (named after the Sylvia Plath short story), who recorded it as 'Not Bitter but Bored' and it was finally released on a compilation with the same name in 2006. With new lyrics by Morrissey and a slightly altered melody, the song would go on to become a Moz classic, in which he deals with all the racism accusations made throughout the years. Morrissey was indeed back – with a vengeance.

'I Have Forgiven Jesus' (Morrissey/Whyte)

Released as the fourth and final single from the album on December 13th 2004, it peaked at #10 in the US, making it Morrissey's fourth top ten single in a row – impressive for an artist that was more or less forgotten only a few years earlier.

So, what could have been yet another controversy for Morrissey, considering the title and theme, was just another hit single. Moz was definitely on a roll here! In the lyrics, he sings directly to the Lord Almighty and says that he forgives him for giving him a lot of needs and desires that he can't give in to because of his catholic upbringing. Whyte's mid-tempo song is a good match to Moz's lyrics, though the arrangement, with the electric piano and what sounds like a drum loop, is a bit out of character for Morrissey. But that never stopped him before.

'Come Back to Camden' (Morrissey/Boorer)

Back in the early-to-mid 90s, Morrissey lived in Camden in North London – the epicentre of the britpop wave sweeping across the UK at the time. He has admitted in later interviews that the song was about 'a particular person', and that person is allegedly Jake Walters, Morrissey's former personal assistant who lived with him for a while in Camden (and there have been a lot of rumours about what kind of relationship the two really had). Unsurprisingly, the lyrics paint a vivid picture of life in Camden ('drinking tea with the taste of the Thames / ... / where taxi drivers never stop talking'), but Morrissey also finds the time to beg for the subject of the song to come back home, as he promises to be good if he or she does so. And he really does sound passionate here. Boorer's sweeping piano ballad is somewhat 'soiled' by those cheap-sounding synth strings, but it's still a really good song.

'I'm Not Sorry' (Morrissey/Boorer)

After forgiving Jesus just a couple of songs ago, Morrissey now says that he doesn't regret the things he has done (which could be quite a lot, really), but of course, he also takes the opportunity to dwell on love that never happened. What would a self-reflecting Moz lyric be without a splash of self-pity? Musically, it sounds a bit like 'Jack the Ripper' (from the 'Certain People I Know' single in 1992), and the flute, played by Rhys Williams, is a nice touch to this great ballad.

'The World Is Full of Crashing Bores' (Morrissey/Boorer)

What could be an album track from Suede's commercial peak from 1996, *Coming Up* is one of the more mediocre songs on this album. The title does sound like one of Morrissey's beloved Oscar Wilde's famous one-liners, but that's probably the most exciting thing about this track. As always, he ends up longing for love ('take me in your arms and love me'), and before that, he's managed to wag his finger at both pop stars (who are 'thicker than pig shit') and the law enforcement. Despite all this, it's one of the few songs off the album that's been a constant in Morrissey's live shows since its release.

'How Can Anybody Possibly Know How I Feel?' (Morrissey/Whyte)

Morrissey normally isn't one to swear or use foul words in his lyrics, but here it actually happens in two songs in a row, as the word 'shit' appears in both this and the previous track (the first two songs in his entire career to contain the word). This was probably one of his bluntest and ugliest lyrics so far, and as well as the s-word, he continues with another theme from the song above, once again attacking people with authority in 'smelly' uniforms. Well, Morrissey was feeling outraged and alone, and he thought that he might write a song about it, which wasn't a brilliant idea in hindsight. The *Southpaw Grammar* period rock sound doesn't do the song much favour either, I'm afraid.

'First of the Gang to Die' (Morrissey/Whyte)

Released as the second single off the album in July 2004, it became an instant hit in the UK, where it peaked at #6, making it Morrissey's second top ten hit in a row there. It's also a return to the classic 'character' theme that he'd explored a lot earlier on in his solo career. In this song, we get to know Hector, a young Latino, whose criminal lifestyle makes him... well, the first of the gang to die. Its sing-along chorus may be a bit odd, considering the lyrics, but it's impossible to deny the impact of this song. At this time, Whyte surely knew how to keep those hit singles coming! Apart from being a hit single in his home country, it's also the song Moz has sung live most in his entire catalogue since 2002, when he premiered it in concert (although the music was older than that, as Whyte recorded the song as 'Stay With Me' with his band, Johnny Panic and the Bible of Dreams, in the 1990s). The Latino theme in the lyrics also came after he discovered that he was an idol in the Hispanic community. Latinos can probably relate to Morrissey's outsider view, having historically felt like outcasts in their own country. This new acquaintance would result in the 1999/2000 tour, called 'Oy Esteban!' (which is Spanish for 'Hey Steven!') The *NME* would, seven years later, place the song at #147 on their list of the 150 best tracks of the past fifteen years.

'Let Me Kiss You' (Morrissey/Whyte)

This was the third song released as a single from the album on October 11th 2004 (peaking at #8 in the UK) and was originally written for Nancy Sinatra. Oddly enough, she released her own version as a single on the same day, on the same label (Attack), and with Moz on backing vocals. Nancy's single peaked at #46. The song itself is more or less a standard Whyte mid-tempo track, in which Morrissey once again turns to self-pity and self-loathing, begging the subject of the song to close his or her eyes, and think of someone they are more attracted to before kissing him.

'All the Lazy Dykes' (Morrissey/Whyte)

What might appear from the title to be a stab at the lesbian community is rather a celebration of it. Morrissey has said in interviews that he got the inspiration for the lyrics from passing the iconic lesbian hangout, Palms Bar, on Santa Monica Boulevard in his new hometown of Los Angeles. There he saw what he described as a 'fascinating clientele' of 'very, very strong women'. He also said that he wrote the song to help a friend of his to take the step and come out of the closet and be herself. It's quite far from being among the top tracks of this album, though.

'I Like You' (Morrissey/Boorer)
I guess many Morrissey fans wondered what was happening when this track came on, as it kicks off with some synthesizer noises (that keeps appearing throughout the song), before evolving into... well, a standard Morrissey/Boorer tune. Apparently, Robbie Williams took a liking to this song, as he suggested that he and Moz should perform it as a duet at the 2005 Brit Awards, but he was turned down. It's been suggested that the lyrics, which are a hymn to a friend, are about Johnny Marr, but then again, most fans think every song that mentions a lost friend is about his former songwriting partner, so you probably shouldn't take it too seriously. And of course, he takes the opportunity to take another stab at the British courts, this time the magistrates. I really hoped that 'Sorrow Will Come in the End' would be the end of that...

'You Know I Couldn't Last' (Morrissey/Boorer/Day)
The closing track of the album (it was also released as a 2CD deluxe edition, but this was the original closer) is co-written by bassist Gary Day, Morrissey, and Boorer, and it's quite obvious that they all wanted to come up with the perfect farewell, as it's by far the longest track on the record, with a shifting temperament that goes from piano ballad verses to indie rock choruses. Lyrically, it's kind of a return to the old 'Paint a Vulgar Picture' theme, as he once again bashes the music industry and all the money the labels make on records and merchandise. He also feels that the tables have turned and that now he's the pop star fading into obscurity ('the teenagers who love you, they will wake up, yawn and kill you'). And does he insist on one final stab at the legal system? Of course!

'Don't Make Fun of Daddy's Voice' (Morrissey/Whyte)
Released as a B-side on the 'Let Me Kiss You' single, this is probably one of the weirdest and most unexpected songs in the entire Morrissey catalogue, but it's wise to bear in mind that the music was another one originally written for Whyte's band, Johnny Panic and the Bible of Dreams (who recorded it as 'Paranoia'), a band that was more into indie rock than Moz has ever been. The lyrics are basically just as unexpected, as it tells the story of a kid who's poking fun at his or her father's voice, which is sounding a bit weird because something got stuck in his throat when he was younger. Oh, we have come a long way from 'There's a Light That Never Goes Out' here...

'It's Hard to Walk Tall When You're Small' (Morrissey/Whyte)
After the indie rock blast of the previous song, Morrissey keeps on walking down the very same path on this one, originally released as the B-side to 'Irish

Blood, English Heart'. The lyrics, in which Morrissey finds it appropriate to have a stab at short people, were actually written for a song that was meant to be included on the B-side to 'Satan Rejected My Soul'. But after recording the backing track and some vocals, the song (which was then written by drummer Cobrin) was canned, for some reason. Maybe because it just wasn't very good?

'Teenage Dad on His Estate' (Morrissey/Whyte)

After two rather dismal B-sides, this one is actually quite good. Originally released on the 'First of the Gang to Die' single, this is a step away from the misplaced grunge rock of the previous two tracks, and we're suddenly back in more classic Morrissey land with this mid-tempo Whyte song. The lyrics are quite funny as well: someone is looking down on a man who hasn't got a lot of money and lives in a modest home, but he's still happier (and he apparently owns a Jensen Interceptor, which is a sports car that was made in the UK in the 40s and 70s). The first verse ('You marry because it's expected of you / And it only makes you more lonely') also echoes the old B-side 'Will Never Marry'.

'Munich Air Disaster 1958' (Morrissey/Whyte)

Morrissey's childhood home on Kings Road in Manchester was just a stone's throw away from Old Trafford, Manchester United's home ground, so it is logical that he would be a fan of The Reds. Here, he pays tribute to the plane crash on February 6th 1958, when eight players, eight journalists and several club representatives from Manchester United died when their plane slid off the runway and caught fire on their way home from a European Cup game against Red Star Belgrade. But it's not just a tribute to the casualties – it's also a metaphor for his own life, almost envying those who passed away at the peak of their life. The song was released as the B-side to 'Irish Blood, English Heart', and was often played together with a cover of New York Dolls' 'Subway Train' when played live.

'Friday Mourning' (Morrissey/Whyte)

This gentle piano-based ballad was first released on 'Let Me Kiss You', and it's a quite generic, self-pitying Morrissey song, once again. Apart from the wordplay in the title (which is actually quite clever), the theme here is pretty dark, as Morrissey remembers all the people (teachers, parents and bosses) who have called him a loser throughout the years. The song is often compared to 'Late Night Maudlin Street' (from *Viva Hate*), which isn't that strange, as the two songs share both arrangement and theme, in a way.

'The Never-Played Symphonies' (Morrissey/Whyte)

As usual, when we're talking piano ballads, the writer here is Whyte (he actually wrote all the B-sides here, apart from 'Mexico'), and when listening to it, you really wonder why Morrissey decided to keep this off the album, and instead put it on the 'Irish Blood, English Heart' B-side. This would actually have been one of my favourite songs on the album. Here, Morrissey is contemplating his life whilst on his deathbed, and while he thinks about all the people who have loved or put up with him, he would rather focus on the ones he never had sex with. It all ends with a sound of a gong for maximum dramatic effect.

'My Life Is a Succession of People Saying Goodbye' (Morrissey/Whyte)
Once again, Morrissey appears to be singing from his deathbed, this time contemplating on all the people he has lost in his life and wondering what's left for him. Released on the 'First of the Gang to Die' single, this is the fifth ballad in a row, following the first couple of rockers, and it's also another piano-based song, though the arrangement was enhanced by the addition of a harp, played by Camilla Pay.

'I Am Two People' (Morrissey/Whyte)
In an interview in 2004, Morrissey reflected on his star sign, Gemini, and concluded that he was indeed two people, 'one gregarious and one impossibly shy', and later that year, he released this song on the same theme, first released as the B-side to 'Let Me Kiss You'. In the lyrics, he takes the aforementioned thoughts about his dual personality and takes it one step further, by adding that there is 'One you know – but don't like / The other one, you don't know / But you don't want to'. Musically, this is yet another standard Whyte song, with some nice piano playing by Michael Farrell.

'Mexico' (Morrissey/Boorer/Day)
As I mentioned earlier on, Morrissey discovered that he had a substantial following in the Latino community, and especially in Mexico; therefore, it was only fair that he would end up writing a tribute to his new favourite country – this time with the help of both Boorer and Gary Day, who composed this soft and sweeping tune. Along with the celebration of Mexico, he also adds some more anti-American views, commenting on the harsh Texan border controls. The song was one of the new songs premiered during the 2002 tour, but it never made it to the album and had to settle for a place on the 'First of the Gang to Die' single. Needless to say, this has become a live favourite, especially when he plays in the Latino countries.

Contemporary Singles
Redondo Beach (live) (single, 2005)
Personnel:
Morrissey: vocals
Boz Boorer: guitar, congas, backing vocals
Jesse Tobias: guitar
Gary Day: bass guitar

Dean Butterworth: drums
Michael Farrell: keyboards, trumpet, backing vocals

'Redondo Beach' (Patti Smith/Richard Sohl/Lenny Kaye)
This single was released to promote the live album *Live at Earls Court*, recorded in London on December 18th 2004, and released on April 4th 2005 in the UK. It came as no surprise that Morrissey decided to cover this Patti Smith song (originally released on her classic *Horses* album in 1975), as hc had been talking about how important that album was to him for years. His version of the song sounds quite a lot like the original recording, even copying the faux-reggae arrangement, but he gets the opening line wrong (he sings 'let it be known' instead of 'late afternoon', though you can't really blame him, as Patti's vocals aren't very audible).

'There's a Light That Never Goes Out' (live) (Morrissey/Marr)
This was probably the reason why the single got to #11 in the UK, even though this live rendition of the old Smiths classic is played a bit too slowly. But the audience doesn't seem to mind.

Live at Earls Court (live album, 2005)

Personnel:
Morrissey: vocals
Boz Boorer: guitar, congas, clarinet, backing vocals
Jesse Tobias: guitar
Gary Day: bass guitar
Dean Butterworth: drums
Michael Farrell: keyboards, percussion, trumpet, backing vocals
Jed Weitzman: photography
Produced by Peter Asher
Playing time: 74:11
Label: Sanctuary (UK/US)
Release date: April 4th 2005 (UK), March 29th 2005 (US)
Highest chart position: UK: 18, US: 119

Thirteen years after his first live album, *Beethoven Was Deaf*, Morrissey finally released a second one, recorded mostly at Earls Court in London on December 18th 2004, although some of the tracks were taken from shows earlier on the tour. This was the CD equivalent of the live DVD, *Who Put The M In Manchester*, which was recorded during the same tour in Manchester in May 2004.

In contrast to the earlier live album, this one does include some Smiths songs (like 'How Soon Is Now?', 'Bigmouth Strikes Again' and 'Shoplifters Of The World Unite'), and also some older songs from his own solo catalogue, like 'November Spawned A Monster' and 'The More You Ignore Me, The Closer I Get'. He also manages to squeeze in two covers, Patti Smith's 'Redondo Beach' (see previous single entry) and 'Subway Train' by New York Dolls, which is played as a medley with his own 'Munich Air Disaster 1958'.

The album made it to #18 in the UK, but the sales in the US were far more disappointing, peaking at #119.

Ringleader of the Tormentors (2006)

Personnel:
Morrissey: vocals, art direction
Boz Boorer: guitars
Alain Whyte: guitars, backing vocals
Jesse Tobias: guitars
Gary Day: bass guitar
Matt Chamberlain: drums
Michael Farrell: piano, organ, keyboards, trumpet, trombone, percussion
Ennio Morricone: string arrangement (on 'Dear God Please Help Me')
Fabio Lovino: photography
Recorded at Forum Music Village (Rome, Italy)
Produced by Tony Visconti
Playing time: 50:05
Label: Sanctuary/Attack (UK)
Release date: April 3 2006
Highest chart position: UK: 1, US: 27

So, Morrissey came back with a vengeance on *You Are the Quarry*, with four consecutive top 10 singles in the UK, and a successful tour following it as well. Was he able to follow up this triumphant return? There had been a lot of speculation on whether *Quarry* was Morrissey's fond farewell to his fans and the music scene, but he would soon prove that those rumours were far from true.

Since the release of *You Are the Quarry*, Morrissey had been on tour, and he had also decided to leave Los Angeles, instead settling in Italy's capital, Rome. The new environment proved to be exactly what Moz needed to get things going again, and he quickly wrote a bunch of songs for the next album.

During the tour, guitarist Alain Whyte suddenly quit the band, supposedly after suffering a nervous breakdown (it would soon turn out that he was still a part of the backing band in the studio and had continued to write songs), which meant they had to find a replacement guitarist for the live dates. They soon found Jesse Tobias, an American guitarist who had played in Red Hot Chili Peppers for a short while and then toured with Alanis Morrissette for six years, before joining the former Smiths singer in 2004. Tobias would go on to be what some people have called 'Morrissey's muse', and that might be true, as it was quite obvious that Moz became very inspired by Tobias' presence and his contributions both as a musician and a songwriter. As for the rest of the band, Boorer and Day stayed, while drummer Dean Butterworth wanted to focus on his band Good Charlotte, and was replaced by Matt Chamberlain, who had previously played with acts like Pearl Jam, Soundgarden, David Bowie, and Edie Brickell & the New Bohemians.

All he needed now was a producer. Initially, he wanted to enlist Jeff Saltzman, who had just produced a hugely popular album by The Killers

(*Hot Fuss*), but he was very much in demand; so after trying to produce the album within the band, Morrissey convinced iconic producer Tony Visconti (most famous for recording with David Bowie and Marc Bolan, but also Morrissey's old favourites Sparks, among many others) to take a seat in the producer's chair. As Morrissey had found his new paradise in Rome, he decided to stay there to record the album. So, the team settled at Forum Music Village, most famous for being a popular music studio for the Italian movie industry. This is why iconic soundtrack composer Ennio Morricone was enlisted to score 'Dear God Please Help Me' – because he happened to be at the studio at this time.

When released in April 2006, the album was met with generally very positive reviews, but more importantly – it entered the UK album charts at #1, which was the third Morrissey album to do so (*Viva Hate* and *Vauxhall and I* were the previous two). Speaking of the album title, Morrissey once said that he always felt that he was something of a ringleader for the group of younger guitar pop bands that emerged in the UK in the early 2000s, as they all cited him as a big influence.

Despite the chart success of the album, it failed to deliver hit singles in the same way that *You Are the Quarry* did. The first single, 'You Have Killed Me', peaked at #3, but the remaining three singles barely made it to the top 20. That didn't really matter, though, as Morrissey cemented his comeback with this album, and I guess no one doubted that he was back for good.

'I Will See You in Far Off Places' (Morrissey/Whyte)

If you hoped for a more mellow Morrissey album after the rock-influenced *You Are the Quarry*, then this opening track probably smashed those hopes to bits. As the title indicates, this is Morrissey's own take on the old standard 'We'll Meet Again', with the theme of an afterlife that will be spent together with all your loved ones. He also takes the opportunity to point a finger at the US again, this time commenting on their bomb attacks in the Middle East ('Blair and Bush are not terrorism, they're worse than terrorism', he said in interviews at the time). Musically, this is a very powerful album opener, with its slow and rumbling rhythm, which might seem a bit repetitive on first listen, but it's a grower.

'Dear God, Please Help Me' (Morrissey/Whyte)

As I mentioned earlier, Morrissey really found his paradise when moving to Rome, and here he even mentions the city in the first line, as he finds himself walking through the streets with his 'heart on a string'. Apart from the beautiful arrangement of this grand ballad, what first really strikes you here are Morrissey's vocals, which are probably better than ever before, and of course, the strings, famously arranged by Mr. Morricone (and it's great to finally hear some real strings, and not just those quite horribly synthesized ones). So, to the lyrics then… well, what can you say? Lines like 'there are explosive kegs between my legs' and 'now I'm spreading your legs, with mine in between, speak for themselves, really. This is a song about sex, and even though many fans interpreted it to be about a gay experience Moz supposedly had in Rome, he has always denied that. I'm not sure that matters, though. Two years later, Marianne Faithful recorded a cover of the song for her album 'Easy Come, Easy Go'.

'You Have Killed Me' (Morrissey/Tobias)

As the first sample from the album, released as a single on March 27 2006 (peaking at #3 in the UK), this was a perfect example of how Morrissey's sound had evolved during the past two years. Written by new guitarist Jesse Tobias, it's an undeniable hit, and it comes as no surprise that it has been on the live setlists since its release. The lyrics are, once again, loaded with sexual references, but he's also name dropping a lot of Italian places and people, like the Piazza Cavour in Rome, directors Pier Paolo Pasolini and Luchino Visconti, and actress Anna Magnani. When playing the song live, Morrissey sometimes swapped Visconti's first name to that of Tony, as a homage to the album's producer. The music video shows Morrissey and his band (where guitarist Alain Whyte sits in on drums instead of Matt Chamberlain) performing the song, in what could be a tribute to Moz's beloved Eurovision Song Contest of the late 60s and early 70s.

'The Youngest Was the Most Loved' (Morrissey/Tobias)

The second single off the album, released on June 5 2006, peaked at #14 in the UK while actually doing even better in the US, where it reached #11 on the singles chart. Just like the previous (and next) single, this one was written by Tobias – but judging from the tune, this could just as well have been written by Alain Whyte. The most ear-catching thing here is probably the children's choir, consisting of seven Italian kids (they would appear on two more songs on the album), that add some occasional backing vocals every now and then. The music video, which features Moz as a convicted criminal being led out of the court by the police (played by his band), echoes the lyrics about a poor young boy who grows up to be a killer. Morrissey was apparently very unhappy with how the single performed in the charts, blaming it all on the label in an email that was leaked on a Morrissey fan website.

'In the Future When All's Well' (Morrissey/Tobias)

The third single in a row on the album, this one was also released as the third single off the album on August 21 2006, peaking at #17 in the UK. Here, Morrissey once again sings about how the afterlife is to be preferred over being alive and kicking, and the final verse of the song also echoes the lyrics to his old Smiths song, 'Asleep', as he states that the 'future is ended by a long, long sleep'. Musically, it's a bit of a nod to producer Visconti's back catalogue, with a clear glam influence.

'The Father Who Must Be Killed' (Morrissey/Whyte)
The children's choir returns for this quite odd entry in the Morrissey lyric catalogue, as he tells the rather poetic story of a girl who kills her own father and then ends up killing herself as well. Whyte's tune goes from being something of a standard pop song to a more upbeat chorus, spiced up with some classic power pop chords. It's probably not one of the most loved songs from the album amongst fans, but it's a nice song that adds to the diversity of the record.

'Life Is a Pigsty' (Morrissey/Whyte)
Morrissey has been seen bursting into tears while singing this one live, and he has also said that this is his personal favourite among his songs, as it pretty much sums up his life, according to the singer. By far the longest track on the album (ending after seven minutes and 22 seconds), this epic tale of how the whole world is, well, a pigsty, is surprisingly monotonous, but considering the subject of the song, it might be fitting, after all. Producer Visconti once called it a 'suite', rather than a 'song', and there's a bit of truth in that – but it's far from exciting enough to be compared to the work of the classic composers.

'I'll Never Be Anybody's Hero Now' (Morrissey/Whyte)
Another song filled to the rim with Morrissey's self-pity, where he, among other things, mourns that his one true love is 'under the ground' and that he thinks of himself as a ghost, as people seem to walk right through him. It can't be easy being Morrissey, that's for sure. The song itself isn't really something to write home about, though Morrissey delivers some of his best vocals on the album!

'On the Streets I Ran' (Morrissey/Tobias)
Already, in the first notes, you can hear that this is one of the songs Morrissey wrote with Tobias for this album, with its more rock-based sound, and combination of jangly guitars and power chords. The singer admitted in an interview at the time of the album's release that the song was a result of his own frequent thoughts about death, and in the lyrics, he even finds out that he will leave this world on a Thursday. This is the only Tobias song on the album that didn't end up as a single, and that was probably for the best. It's not a bad song, but it just seems a bit bland. That being said, it's good to finally have an up-tempo song after a sequence of slow-paced ones.

'To Me You Are a Work of Art' (Morrissey/Whyte)
For once, Morrissey doesn't turn to self-pity, even though he manages to squeeze in a tiny portion of it anyway in the line: 'I would give you my heart / that's if I had one.' Here he opts for praising someone he would gladly give his heart to. He also finds the time to let us know that seeing the world around him makes him ill. This is probably Whyte's best contribution to the album, with its memorable guitar line, and nice pop melody.

'I Just Want To See the Boy Happy' (Morrissey/Tobias)
The fourth and final single released from the album (on December 6 2006, peaking at #16 in the UK), and another Tobias composition, more reminiscent of the *Southpaw Grammar* days than the Moz style at the time (except maybe for the Mariachi trumpet, courtesy of Michael Farrell, that comes in towards the end of the song). In the lyrics, Morrissey once again turns to God, telling him that he's willing to sacrifice his own life in order to satisfy 'the boy'. Some fans probably wondered if the Holy Moz had turned religious in his old age…

'At Last I Am Born' (Morrissey/Farrell)
The Italian kids return for their third and final appearance on this closing song, written with keyboard player Michael Farrell (he only co-wrote one more song with Morrissey, the later B-side, 'Sweetie-Pie'). As we established earlier, Morrissey really enjoyed his new hometown of Rome, and here he hints at being born again in the Italian capital, summarizing his life in the line: 'from troubled child to spectral hand to Claude Brasseur' (Brasseur is a French actor, who starred in movies by Jean-Luc Godard and François Truffaut in the 60s). In contemporary interviews, he added that 2005 and 2006 had been really good years for him and that he had finally realised a lot of things about his life. Musically, it's a fitting album closer, with its theatrical and dramatic arrangement. The piano plays an important role, together with some flamenco-inspired guitars and the aforementioned children's choir.

Years of Refusal (2009)

Personnel:
Morrissey: vocals
Boz Boorer: guitars
Jesse Tobias: guitars
Solomon Walker: bass guitar
Matt Walker: drums
Michael Farrell: keyboards, accordion
Roger Manning: keyboards
Jake Walters: photography (front photo)
Travis Shinn: photography (band photo)
No Allegiances: sleeve
Recorded at Conway Recording Studios (Los Angeles, USA)
Produced by Jerry Finn
Seth Waldmann: engineer
Playing time: 43:25
Label: Decca (UK), Lost Highway (US)
Release date: February 16 2009
Highest chart position: UK: 3, US: 11

After recording *Ringleader of the Tormentors* in Rome in 2006, Morrissey spent the next couple of years touring the US and Europe, and in the gap between the tours, he summoned the band to Los Angeles, where they recorded the next album, from August 2007 until late spring 2008. But of course, there had been some changes, and this time Gary Day had left as bass player, being replaced by Solomon Walker, whose brother Matt had replaced Matt Chamberlain as the drummer during the tour (Matt Walker previously played with The Smashing Pumpkins, and Garbage, among others). Keyboardist Michael Farrell also left during the recording of the album, and Roger Manning (who played on *You Are the Quarry*) stepped in to replace him for the rest of the recording. So, what happened to Alain Whyte? Well, he wrote five of the songs on the album but doesn't appear on the recordings at all.

Apart from a few new band members, Morrissey also decided to work with a different producer, as Jerry Finn came back to the studio to work on this album. Finn produced Moz's big 'comeback album', *You Are the Quarry*, and he obviously wanted to find that spark again. Funnily enough, Tony Visconti said in an interview early on that he would produce the next Morrissey album as well, but I guess the singer had one of his famous changes of mind.

So, with all these new team members, all he needed now was a label. He was once again without one – this is something that would haunt Morrissey for the next decade or so – when Sanctuary was sold to mega major label Universal, so it was more a question of what Universal sub-label he would end up on. Having a fondness for old iconic brands, he came to the classic Decca label, who released a *Greatest Hits* album in February 2008, mostly containing songs from his last two albums and two new songs (did anybody say 'Paint a Vulgar Picture'?). The new songs ended up on *Years of Refusal*, and he managed to change to Polydor before the album was released.

Originally planned for release in September 2008, the album finally came out in February 2009 and was mostly praised by the critics at the time. Nowadays, the record has divided the Moz fans into two camps – those that think it's one of his best albums ever, and those that really don't care much for it at all.

Many fans reacted to the somewhat bizarre cover photo, which shows Morrissey holding a baby in his arms. The baby was Sebastien Pesel-Browne, the son of Morrissey's assistant tour manager Charlie Browne, and the photo was taken by Jake Walters, Morrissey's former personal assistant and roomie.

'Something Is Squeezing My Skull' (Morrissey/Whyte)

This punk rocker is an excellent opener for this album, with Morrissey really showing off his vocal skills (especially the way he sings the word 'skull' in the chorus). It was released as the fourth and final single off the album on April 27 2009, peaking at #46 in the UK singles chart (but actually getting to the top of the Scottish equivalent). The cover art of the single shows Morrissey posing with the Johnny Ramone memorial at the Hollywood Forever Cemetery, which is actually quite appropriate for this song, both musically and lyrically, as he deals with the heavy focus on medication (or sedation, to make the Ramones connection more visible) in modern society.

'Mama Lay Softly on the Riverbed' (Morrissey/Whyte)

At first glance, this song is apparently about someone's mother who has committed suicide, but Morrissey also pokes a few sturdy fingers at the people who he thinks drove her to do it. Was it 'the pigs in grey suits'? Or the 'priggish moneymen'? If this had been a song solely about suicide, it would probably have been a much softer affair (like 'I Know It's Over'), but since the lyrics also contain a lot of anger, the rock arrangement suits it quite well. The music was written by Whyte, and the song was first played during the tour that preceded the recording sessions.

'Black Cloud' (Morrissey/Boorer)

This song about unrequited love features one of the most unlikely guest appearances ever on a Morrissey song, as guitar virtuoso Jeff Beck briefly joins the band. In an interview with music magazine *Mojo* at the time of the album's release, Beck explained that he had met Morrissey and his friend Chrissie Hynde (of the Pretenders, who's also on this album) at a bar in Los Angeles and that Morrissey had asked Hynde to invite Beck to play on the album, as he was too shy to ask himself. Morrissey left him a CD the next day, and then they recorded the track in a few hours in the studio. The song opens in a promising way, with a child softly asking: 'Can you see the black cloud?', with Beck then entering with some nice guitar lines. He is soon interrupted, though, by some clumsy *Southpaw Grammar* style rock, which is a shame, really.

'I'm Throwing My Arms Around Paris' (Morrissey/Boorer)
There is a rumour saying that this song was originally written to become the UK entry in the 2007 Eurovision Song Contest, with Morrissey as the performer, but since he didn't get it in in time for consideration, the song never even got into the selection process, which was instead won by Scooch's 'Flying The Flag (For You)'. I'm not sure how true this is, but eventually, the song was released as the first single taken from the album (not counting the two singles released from the 'Greatest Hits' album in 2008) on February 9 2009, peaking at #21 in the UK (and once again topping the Scottish singles chart). Lyrically, he abandoned his old flame Rome and was now aiming his love at the French capital instead, which might not come as a surprise for his old fans, bearing in mind his life-long love of Oscar Wilde (who died in Paris in November 1900 and is buried there). For this Paris tribute, Boorer wrote what could easily be described as a classic pop song, clocking in at two minutes and 30 seconds, making it the perfect single. Too bad it didn't make more of an impression on the charts.

'All You Need Is Me' (Morrissey/Tobias)
Originally released as one of two new songs on the *Greatest Hits* album in 2008, it was also issued as a single at the time, peaking at #24 in June 2008 (it was only available in stores for one week). Here, Jesse Tobias is back with his first song of the album, and as usual for him, we're back in punk/rock country mode, while Morrissey allegedly sings about how his fans groan, moan and roll their eyes to the sky when talking about him, but they're still by his side. Because all we need is him, apparently, but he leaves us with the line 'you're gonna miss me when I'm gone', and that might very well be true.

'When Last I Spoke To Carol' (Morrissey/Whyte)
The flamenco style opening riff is just a teaser of what's to come in this song, as legendary trumpeter Mark Isham – Morrissey's first choice, Herb Alpert, wasn't available for the recording session – who had previously worked with names like Van Morrison, XTC and Joni Mitchell, makes his entrance. The lyrics concern a woman, born in 1975, who loves the singer. Sadly, he doesn't feel the same about her and ends up saying goodbye to her while her casket is being lowered into the ground. Bleak words, but once again, the music doesn't really match their darkness, even though the wind blowing in the outro resembles the bleakness of the classic Smiths song 'Asleep'.

'That's How People Grow Up' (Morrissey/Boorer)
Boz Boorer had been waiting patiently to have one of his songs released as a single (his last one to this point was 'Satan Rejected My Soul' in 1997), and

now it finally happened. The song was originally one of the two new songs on the *Greatest Hits* album in 2008, and this was the first single to be released from it, on February 4 2008, more than a year before *Years of Refusal* came out (the single peaked at #14 in the UK). Kicking off with some opera-style vocals, courtesy of Kristeen Young (who had previously worked with David Bowie and former producer Tony Visconti, and also joined Moz as an opening act on the *Ringleaders* tour), the song then turns into, well, a standard Morrissey song, despite the singer himself calling it his best solo song ever when talking to *People* Magazine in 2009. In the lyrics, he once again turns to self-pity, though admittedly with a pinch of humour as well, and tells the story of how he never seems to find true love. Oh, Moz...

'One Day Goodbye Will Be Farewell' (Morrissey/Boorer)

A common ingredient in the lyrics on this album is Morrissey's hinting that his time as a pop star and as a human being isn't going to last forever. In this case, the title really says it all, and the final line of the song sums it up pretty well: 'One day goodbye will be farewell, so grab me while you still can.' Basically, he's telling his fans to enjoy him while he's still around. The song is pushed forward by Matt Walker's galloping snare drum, and Mark Isham once again returns with his trumpet. It's one of the best songs on this album.

'It's Not Your Birthday Anymore' (Morrissey/Whyte)

Have you found yourself listening to Morrissey's solo efforts, longing for the high-pitched shrieking of the early Smiths days? Well, here's a song for you, then! This is a great example of Morrissey's amazing voice. It's a bit uncomfortable to listen to Moz singing that 'your voice might say 'no'', and then later in the song saying that he's giving the subject of the song 'love' on the floor, 'right here, right now'. But after an album full of rock songs, it's a nice change to have a softer verse, at least, before the distortion pedals and crashing drums appear in time for the chorus. Even though Whyte wasn't part of the recording process anymore, he still kept providing Moz and his band with great tunes, there's no doubt about that.

'You Were Good in Your Time' (Morrissey/Whyte)

For the umpteenth time on this album, Morrissey addresses the thought of not being in this world forever, this time with a person who's about to leave us. It's also an example of 'what you hear isn't always what you'll get', as the song, after a mere three minutes, goes from being a dramatic piano ballad, to become what can only be called an ambient experiment, with swooping electronic sounds, and a sound sample taken from the movie *Pépe Le Moko* (Julien Duvivier, 1937). For me, this is one of the great things about Morrissey – even though he might seem to be very conservative musically (and politically, but that's a totally different story), he still surprises his fans again and again.

'Sorry Doesn't Help' (Morrissey/Tobias)

Tobias is back, and with him, the stodgy rock setting that we have come to know by now. Many Moz fans supposed that this was another song dealing with the infamous Court Case thirteen years earlier, probably because he mentions a QC in the first verse; but since he's also singing about his teen years, I would guess that, for once, he isn't singing about his legal battle with Mike Joyce (and the drummer has hardly asked for forgiveness). More likely, this is Morrissey's way of saying that he won't forgive those who have mistreated him in the past. And his voice is once again marvellous!

'I'm OK by Myself' (Morrissey/Tobias)

The last song of the original album (there were two bonus tracks added to the digital version on iTunes in the US), this is something of a resignation from Morrissey – after all the lost and unrequited loves throughout the years, he's singing (and howling) that he's actually okay by himself, and that it may come as a shock for us to hear that. For a Tobias song, it's actually quite nuanced, even though it's rather furious at the same time. But enough talk about the music and lyrics – the main attraction here is the vocal. Moz is both showing off his great voice for a final time on this record and howling his way through the last minutes of the song. Apparently, producer Finn didn't like the song, but it still made it to the album. I'm glad it did.

'Because of My Poor Education' (Morrissey/Whyte)

Originally released as the B-side to the 'I'm Throwing My Arms Around Paris' single, this song was added as a bonus track on the US digital release on Apple's iTunes platform. In the lyrics, Morrissey tries to blame his lack of true love on his poor education, which doesn't really make much sense. Music-wise, it's one of the more mellow songs recorded during the album sessions, with Whyte delivering yet another of his trademark piano ballads.

'Shame Is the Name' (Morrissey/Whyte)

The second iTunes bonus track was also released on the 'Paris' single and features both backing vocals from Chrissie Hynde (of The Pretenders) and a sound sample from Francois Truffaut's *The 400 Blows (Les Quatre Cents Coups)* from 1959. In the lyrics, Morrissey concludes that 'shame makes the world go round' after scolding dumb teens who drink until they throw up, and politicians who spend more money on war than on the elderly back home. Musically, it's one of Whyte's best songs on the album, with some really nice touches of piano and harmonica throughout the song.

Swords (compilation, 2009)

Personnel:
Morrissey: vocals
Alain Whyte: guitars
Boz Boorer: guitars
Jesse Tobias: guitars
Gary Day: bass guitar
Solomon Walker: bass guitar
Matt Walker: drums
Dean Butterworth: drums
Matt Chamberlain: drums
Michael Farrell: keyboards
Roger Manning Jr: keyboards
Kristeen Young: backing vocals
Chrissie Hynde: backing vocals
Morrissey: photography (band photos)
Travis Shinn: photography (front photo)
Glen Nakasako: sleeve
Produced by Jerry Finn, Tony Visconti and Gustavo Santaolalla
Playing time: 67:47
Label: Polydor
Release date: October 26th 2009
Highest chart position: UK:–, US:–

Much like the earlier compilation *Bona Drag* (1990), *Swords* was released to bring all the non-album single B-sides together on one album, mostly for the fans who missed out on the singles, presumably. The Smiths did the same thing in the 80s as well, with *Hatful of Hollow* and The *World Won't Listen*. The B-sides collected here are taken from the singles released for the albums *You Are the Quarry* (2004), *Ringleader of the Tormentors* (2006), and *Years of Refusal*, which had come out earlier in 2009. Even though this isn't a complete collection of the B-sides of this period, most of them are here.

The first edition of *Swords* also came with a bonus CD, which contained eight songs recorded at the Stodoola in Warsaw, Poland, on July 7th, 2009 (among the songs was 'Why Don't You Find Out for Yourself' from *Vauxhall and I*).

Morrissey wanted the compilation to be a budget release, much like the aforementioned *Hatful of Hollow* from 1984, but apparently, the label didn't like that idea and sold the record at full price, which disappointed Moz.

After the release of the album, Morrissey went on a short European tour to support it, with dates in the UK, France, the Netherlands, Ireland and Germany. He also played a few shows in the US during that same tour.

'Good Looking Man About Town' (Morrissey/Whyte)

This song, taken from the 'You Have Killed Me' single (released in March 2006), sees Whyte returning to the oriental feeling of 'I Will See You in Far-Off

Places' (from *Ringleader of the Tormentors*), with its repetitive rhythm, and middle-eastern sounds lurking in the background. In the lyrics, Morrissey tries to lure the objects of his desires into bed with him, but as usual, he ends up spending the nights alone.

'Don't Make Fun of Daddy's Voice' (Morrissey/Whyte)
(see *You Are the Quarry* album)

'If You Don't Like Me, Don't Look At Me' (Morrissey/Tobias)
When Tobias entered the stage as a songwriter, he also brought his own form of stodgy rockers. Sure, both Whyte and Boorer had written their fair share of rock tunes in the past, but they were often not as heavy in the wrong way. This song, taken from 'The Youngest Was the Most Loved' single (released in June 2006), is definitely one of them. And maybe Morrissey is talking to his fans when he sings about finding someone else to 'take your gaze away'?

'Ganglord' (Morrissey/Whyte)
Producer Tony Visconti has said in interviews that this was one of his favourite songs from the 'Ringleaders' album sessions. But instead of being included on the album, the song ended up on the B-side to 'The Youngest Was the Most Loved', which feels like a throwaway, to be honest. Apparently, Whyte experimented a lot with repetitive rhythms and chords during this period, as this is yet another one of those songs (like 'Good Looking Man About Town' and 'I Will See You in Far-Off Places'). Lyrically, we hear a criminal's plea to a ganglord to protect him from the police (supposedly in Morrissey's hometown of Los Angeles, as their motto 'to protect and to serve' is mentioned in the lyrics), who just wants to kick him back to the ghetto.

'My Dearest Love' (Morrissey/Whyte)
This B-side, originally released on the 7' version of the 'All You Need Is Me' single, was produced by Gustavo Santaolalla, who is probably best known for composing the Academy Award-winning score to *Brokeback Mountain* in 2005, and *Babel* in 2006. Lyrically, it's classic Morrissey (which finds him looking for true love for a hundred years without success), but Whyte's music is far better, with its dominant piano and organ and pulsating drum beat. In his book *Mozipedia*, author Simon Goddard compares the intro of the song to EMF's hopefully forgotten 1990 hit 'Unbelievable', and he's not that far off, actually.

'The Never-Played Symphonies' (Morrissey/Whyte)
(see *You Are the Quarry* album)

'Sweetie-Pie' (Morrissey/Farrell)
If you by any chance should find Morrissey a bit too predictable musically, I would recommend a listen to this song, taken from the 'I Just Want To See The

Boy Happy' single (released in December 2006). It was written by keyboardist Michael Farrell, and he intended it to be a beautiful piano ballad, which was how it was originally recorded for the *Ringleaders* album (although, to be fair, the piano was joined by guitars and drums about halfway through the song). Somewhere along the way, though, Morrissey changed his mind and decided to make a weird remix of the song with sound effects, with Kristeen Young joining in on backing 'vocals'. The original recording eventually leaked on the internet in 2009, and it seems most fans prefer the saner version of the song.

'Christian Dior' (Morrissey/Boorer)

This was the only song written by Boorer for the *Ringleaders* album, and it didn't even make it to the album; the formerly prolific songwriter now had stiff competition from new boy Tobias! It was originally released on the 'In the Future When All's Well' single in August 2006, and what may look like a tribute to the famous French fashion designer is rather just another song where Morrissey moans through metaphor about his own choices in life, thinking that he could have had a life full of women and alcohol (among other things) had he not chosen the pop star path. Musically, it sounds like a standard Moz mid-tempo song..

'Shame Is the Name' (Morrissey/Whyte)

(see *Years of Refusal* album)

'Munich Air Disaster 1958' (Morrissey/Whyte)

(see *You Are the Quarry* album)

'I Knew I Was Next' (Morrissey/Tobias)

This rather bleak Tobias composition first appeared on the 'You Have Killed Me' single in March 2006, and once again, we find Morrissey moaning about his miserable life. Nobody loves me, etcetera. The only thing that makes it stand out is Michael Farrell's organ, which can be heard every now and then, but that instrument can't carry the song on its own, sadly.

'It's Hard To Walk Tall When You're Small' (Morrissey/Whyte)

(see *You Are the Quarry* album)

'Teenage Dad on His Estate' (Morrissey/Whyte)

(see *You Are the Quarry* album)

'Children in Pieces' (Morrissey/Tobias)

In this song, taken from the 'All You Need Is Me' CD single (released in June 2008), Morrissey turns to Ireland and the industrial schools scandal, during which lots of children were abused for decades until the schools were closed in the 70s. Unlike his earlier lyrics on controversial subjects, Morrissey almost seems to shy away from spelling it out and instead opts for a milder approach, in a sense. Sure, he sings about the school authorities 'kicking the shit' out of the children, but considering all the horrible things that happened at the schools, he could have gone a lot further, which would have been in keeping with his own tradition. Tobias' riff-heavy rock backing is weirdly unfitting to the lyrics as well, and an atmospheric piano tune would have been a lot better here. The song was one of two produced by film scorer Gustavo Santaolalla (the other one being 'My Dearest Love', also on this compilation).

'Friday Mourning' (Morrissey/Whyte)
(see *You Are the Quarry* album)

'My Life Is a Succession of People Saying Goodbye' *(Morrissey/Whyte)*
(see *You Are the Quarry* album)

'Drive-In Saturday' (Live) (David Bowie)
This David Bowie cover was recorded live at the Orpheum Theater in Omaha on May 11, 2007, and was originally found on the 'All You Need Is Me' 7' single. Morrissey first performed the song in New York in February 2000 but then decided to drop it from the repertoire just as quickly as he had introduced it, as the audience really didn't seem to enjoy it. That didn't stop him from going at it again in 2007, with a few changes to Bowie's lyrics (for example, he changed the reference to Mick Jagger to David Johansen of New York Dolls), but the audience still didn't like it, so he dropped the song once again.

'Because of My Poor Education' (Morrissey/Whyte)
(see *Years of Refusal* album)

'Slum Mums' (Morrissey/Boorer/Day)
Taken from the 'I Have Forgiven Jesus' CD single (released in December 2004), this song was only included on the promotional and downloadable copies of this compilation, although it's not listed on the sleeve, which begs the question if it was supposed to be on the official release but then dropped? Anyway, much like on 'Teenage Dad on His Estate', also recorded during the *You Are the Quarry* sessions and later released on the 'First of the Gang To Die' single, Morrissey sings about society's contempt for the slum mums and 'trash'; the Labour government doesn't care about them, and they're not worth a penny. He finally advises the mothers to commit suicide together with their many children, as they will probably be better off that way. On the 'Jesus' single sleeve, Jesse Tobias is credited as the guitarist, which would make it one of his first appearances on a Morrissey recording.

'Human Being' (David Johansen/Johnny Thunders)
The second cover version on the compilation, this one was originally written and recorded by Morrissey's favourite band New York Dolls, who released it on

their second album, 'Too Much Too Soon' in 1974. Moz released his rendition, which is arranged much like the Dolls' recording, on the 'You Have Killed Me' CD single (March 2006), and it features Boz Boorer on saxophone, as well as guitar by both Whyte and Tobias. This is the second of the 'bonus tracks' added to the promotional and downloadable versions of *Swords*.

Interim Singles

Glamorous Glue (single, 2011)

Personnel:
Morrissey: vocals
Boz Boorer: guitars
Alain Whyte: guitars
Gary Day: bass guitar
Spencer Cobrin: drums

'Glamorous Glue' (Morrissey/Whyte)

Originally released on the 'Your Arsenal' album, it never came out as a single at the time, even though a music video was made for the song. Instead, it was released as a single on April 18 2011, to promote the *Very Best of Morrissey* compilation. It peaked at #69 in the UK, making it Morrissey's lowest charting single.

'Treat Me Like a Human Being' (Demo) (Morrissey/Street)

(see *Viva Hate*)

'Safe Warm Lancashire Home' (Demo) (Morrissey/Street)

Just like the previous song, this is also a demo recording made for *Viva Hate* in 1987, but the song was eventually thrown on the scrapheap when Morrissey and Stephen Street wrote far better songs for that album. And you have to agree with them, really. The demo sounds a lot like a rough sketch of a song that probably wouldn't have made it to the album anyway. Drummer Paresi told author Simon Goddard in 2003 that they made a proper recording of the song, but that Moz then decided that he didn't want to use it.

Satellite of Love (live) (single, 2013)

Personnel:
Morrissey: vocals
Boz Boorer: guitars, mixing
Jesse Tobias: guitars
Solomon Walker: bass guitar
Gustavo Manzur: piano, backing vocals
Matt Walker: drums

'Satellite of Love' (Lou Reed)

Recorded live on November 25th 2011, during Morrissey's show at the

Chelsea Ballroom in Las Vegas, this Lou Reed cover was released as a single on December 2, 2013, to commemorate Reed's death on October 27 that same year. The initial release was digital-only, but was later followed by physical releases on 7' and 12' vinyl with additional bonus tracks. The single actually made it to the top of the *Billboard* Hot Singles chart, making it his first US #1 ever, though it's arguable as to whether this was a 'proper' chart-topper, as *Billboard* at this time was counting all kinds of figures, like radio plays, digital and physical sales. As usual, when covering his old heroes, Morrissey stays true to the original, with Manzur's piano carrying the melody (he also sings David Bowie's backing vocals during the last chorus). In some instances, though, he has altered the lyrics – singing 'I cannot stand the TV,' instead of 'I love to watch things on TV'.

'You're Gonna Need Someone on Your Side' (Morrissey/Nevin)
(see *Your Arsenal*)

'Vicar in a Tutu' (live) (Morrissey/Marr)
Originally released on *The Queen Is Dead* in 1986, this song was played by Morrissey on his 2008 tour, and this recording was made during his show in London's Hyde Park on July 4 that year. The Smiths arrangement is more or less intact, with Jesse Tobias jangling away quite nicely.

'You Say You Don't Love Me' (live) (Pete Shelley)
Morrissey's live cover of this delightfully punky pop song by Bolton's finest, Buzzcocks, was recorded during the same show in Hyde Park as the previous song. Unsurprisingly, the song suits Morrissey's rock-loving band fine, but it still feels a bit uninspired to me. Maybe we should be happy that he didn't choose to record it for the *California Son* album a few years later.

'All You Need Is Me' (live) (Morrissey/Tobias)
Yet another one recorded at the Hyde Park show, this song was originally recorded for the *Greatest Hits* album in 2008 and later also appeared on the 2009 album *Years of Refusal*. Since the song was brand new at the time of the concert, the arrangement is identical to the studio version.

'Mama Lay Softly on the Riverbed' (live) (Morrissey/Whyte)
This live version was only available on the digital release of the single and was recorded in Hyde Park, just like the previous tracks. At the time of the show, in July 2008, the song was yet to be released, so this was a sneak peek from the forthcoming album, which came out in 2009. The live version doesn't differ audibly from the studio version in this case.

World Peace Is None of Your Business (album, 2014)

Personnel:
Morrissey: vocals
Boz Boorer: guitars, QChord, clarinet, saxophone
Jesse Tobias: guitars
Solomon Walker: bass guitar
Matt Walker: drums
Gustavo Manzur: keyboards, piano, organ, synths, trumpet, accordion, flamenco guitar, didgeridoo, QChord, backing vocals
Kristeen Young: backing vocals
Produced by Joe Chiccarelli
Engineered by Maxime Le Guil, Aristide Rosier, Damien Arlot and David Schwerkolt
Donnie Knutson: photography (front photo)
Stefan Bucher: sleeve design
Recorded at La Fabrique (Saint-Rémy-de-Provence, France)
Playing time: 54:55
Label: Harvest (UK and US)
Release date: July 15th 2014
Highest chart position: UK:2, US:14

During the five years that passed between *Years of Refusal*, and this, his tenth solo album, a lot of water passed under the Morrissey bridge. Of course, there was a tour supporting the former album, but then followed a few years of health issues, which started on the *Swords* tour, when he collapsed on stage while playing in Swindon. His health would get worse in the early 2010s when he was first diagnosed with a bleeding ulcer in early 2013, and then a few months later caught double pneumonia, which forced him to cancel the US tour he was on at the time.

In early 2011, Morrissey finished his long-awaited autobiography. In the 1990s, he kept saying that he couldn't write his memoirs until all the people he would mention in the book were dead, but it would take until October 2013 before it hit the shelves all over the world, sporting a hilarious *Penguin Classic* cover. The book gained a lot of rave reviews, but most readers agreed that the first half of the book was amazing, and the second half, which is almost solely about the Mike Joyce court case, was… less amazing.

With the release of the aforementioned *Swords* compilation, Morrissey's contract with the Universal group was fulfilled, and once again, he was on his own. Most fans thought that this was it for Morrissey. But no.

In January 2014, Morrissey announced that he had signed a deal for two albums with major label Capitol, and he once again summoned his band to a recording studio, this time in France. The band looked more or less the same as on the *Years of Refusal* album, with Boz Boorer and Jesse Tobias handling the guitars, Solomon Walker the bass guitar, and his brother Matt hitting the drums. The keyboard spot was now filled by Gustavo Manzur, who made his first appearance with the band on the live cover version of Lou Reed's 'Satellite of Love', which was recorded in Las Vegas in 2011 and released as a single in December 2013. Alain Whyte, who wrote a lot of songs for the *Years of Refusal* album, but didn't perform on it, was now completely out of the picture and didn't contribute at all this time.

Replacing Jerry Finn as producer was Joe Chiccarelli, who had previously worked with acts like Tori Amos, Elton John, The Shins and The White Stripes, and he would prove to be a good choice for Morrissey, as Chiccarelli would go on to produce the next three albums as well.

On release, the album got mixed reviews from the critics, although that didn't stop it from entering the UK album charts at #2. Then suddenly, just a few months after the release date, the album was dropped and deleted from all streaming sites, allegedly due to a disagreement between Morrissey and the Capitol sub-label, Harvest. The controversy is to this date not yet solved, which makes the album quite hard to find these days.

'World Peace Is None of Your Business' (Morrissey/Boorer)

The album opens with the title track, which was also the first teaser, released as a digital single on May 13, 2014, (the first four singles released from the album didn't have a physical release until they all came out on 10' vinyl later in 2014). The title alone tells us that Moz is being more political than he has been for a long while, and here he tells us all to mind our own business, and to not interfere with what the government is doing – just pay your taxes and keep your mouth shut. At the end of the song, he's also lining up a few countries where he thinks that the people *should* be interfering with the government (Brazil, Egypt, Bahrain and Ukraine), saying that every vote is supporting this process of political oppression. Musically, we were also treated to a much lighter and more lush production than the previous albums, which had been heavy and rock-influenced. The music video made for the song, directed by Natalie Johns, showed Morrissey sitting by a piano, reciting the lyrics spoken word-style. He's also suddenly joined by Nancy Sinatra.

'Neal Cassady Drops Dead' (Morrissey/Manzur)

To understand this song, you probably need to know who Neal Cassady was (and it might not even be fully understandable then). Cassady was one of the major figures of the iconic Beat Generation in the 50s, along with Jack Kerouac, William S Burroughs and Allen Ginsberg, among others. They are mainly remembered for their psychedelic and groundbreaking novels and poems. In this song, Morrissey first imagines Cassady's death (he died in 1968) being mourned over by Ginsberg, and then goes on to sing what could only be described as a tribute to the Beat way of writing: with mostly incoherent nonsense ('Tikes full of gripe / Whippersnapper's scurvy / Urchin made of acne'). Producer Chiccarelli said in an interview with *Radio.com* in 2014 that he used to call that bit 'the rap section', which reportedly upset Morrissey. The song is written by Morrissey and keyboardist Manzur, and despite the heavy power chords throughout the song, the production saves it from being too muddy in tone.

'I'm Not a Man' (Morrissey/Tobias)

By far the longest song on the album (almost eight minutes), and it's partly because of the tiptoeing intro, which goes on for almost two of them. The first half of the song follows in the footsteps of the intro, with Morrissey being accompanied by just a keyboard. Then halfway through, the drums kick in and emphasize his aversion towards masculinity. He says that men are those who eat meat, fight in wars, and play hockey. The drums keep pounding away with keyboard noises and screams, and he finishes it all off with the simple question, 'Well, what do you think I am? A man?'

'Istanbul' (Morrissey/Boorer)

Released as the second digital single from the album on May 20, 2014, (and later on the limited edition 10' vinyl compilation of the singles that came out in July), this is a tale of a father searching for his son in the Turkish metropolis, among prostitutes and secret streets. The music was made to fit the lyrics, according to Morrissey's wishes, with cigar box guitars, gongs and lap steel guitars, and you can even hear some field recordings made by guitarist Tobias on location in Istanbul. Just like the music video for the album's title track, the video for 'Istanbul' also shows Morrissey reciting the lyrics in the same spoken-word style while making himself a drink.

'Earth Is the Loneliest Planet' (Morrissey/Manzur)

Keeping with the tradition of the first two singles, this third sample from the album also got an initial digital release on June 3, 2014, and then on the 10' vinyl a month later. The music video also followed in the same footsteps as the previous singles, and now Morrissey is joined by American actor (and fellow animal rights activist) Pamela Anderson, as they stand on the roof of the Capitol Records building in Los Angeles. The song has a slight Latino feel to it, at least the rhythm, and along with a meandering organ and accordion, we are also treated to backing vocals courtesy of Kristeen Young (who toured with Morrissey and sang on 'That's How People Grow Up' on the previous album). The lyrics tell the story of a person who is not comfortable with the gender they were assigned at birth and who, sadly, has to deal with the cruelness of the world.

'Staircase at the University' (Morrissey/Boorer)

This rather horrible tale of an over-achieving student, who decides to end her own life because of the pressure from her father and boyfriend to get good grades, is often considered to be one of the highlights of the album, and it's easy to see why. Despite the dark lyrics, the song is surprisingly upbeat, and the sound is fleshed out with Boorer's clarinet, and some lovely Spanish guitars towards the end of the song. Chiccarelli said in an interview with *radio.com* at the time of the album's release that it was a hard song to get right in the studio, with a lot of different musical sections that needed to fit with each other. He managed to do that quite well in the end.

'The Bullfighter Dies' (Morrissey/Tobias)

Not since *Meat Is Murder* had Morrissey been this outspoken about animal rights in a song, even though he often spoke about his involvement with organisations like PETA in interviews throughout the years. This short little pop song about someone cheering when hearing that a bullfighter died instead of a bull, was released as the fourth digital single from the album on June 17, 2014, (it was also featured on the aforementioned 10' vinyl release), and there was also a 7' single planned to be released in early 2015, which the label decided not to go through with. There were also plans for some more 7' singles to be released from the album, with alternative mixes of several songs as B-sides, but none of these came out. Tobias' tune is surprisingly poppy and light, which is also aided by prominent accordion and trumpet, both courtesy of Manzur. The music video, which is done in the same spoken-word style as the first three singles, features just the trumpet and piano as musical accompaniment.

'Kiss Me a Lot' (Morrissey/Tobias)

This fifth and final single from the album released digitally on March 26th 2015, on the Atom Factory label, was originally meant to be a B-side, but while putting the album together, Morrissey felt that it should be on it after all. This Spanish flavoured song features Manzur on trumpet, and the lyrics are relatively straightforward for a Moz love song, with no sight of self-pity at all! The music video, directed by Morrissey's nephew Sam Esty Rayner (who played a kid supposed to look like a young James Dean in the 'Suedehead' video more than 25 years earlier) is hilariously amateurish, and the footage of barely dressed women posing for the camera while miming to the chorus is really quite tasteless.

'Smiler With Knife' (Morrissey/Tobias)

Presumably taking its title from Geoffrey Chaucer's 'The Knight's Tale' (more specifically the line, 'the smiler with the knife under cloak'), this schizophrenic song starts out with just Morrissey and an acoustic guitar (much like the old B-side 'I Know Very Well How I Got My Name'). Then, in the chorus, the drums and electric guitars make a quick guest appearance, only to disappear just as quickly, and we're back with the acoustic setting again. In the instrumental middle eight, the song shifts tempo and sound, and becomes a 'regular' pop song, while the long outro consists of layered backward guitars. Or is it piano? According to Chiccarelli, they distorted a piano and fed it through a guitar amp, so many of the sounds that do sound like a guitar are indeed a distorted piano! The song tells the story of a man who's been deeply hurt and begs 'the smiler' to press the knife against his skin, concluding that 'sex and love are not the same'.

'Kick the Bride Down the Aisle' (Morrissey/Tobias)

Just like the previous song, this one starts out with just Moz and an acoustic guitar but then turns into a waltz-like tune, with an organ spicing up the sound. Kristeen Young turns up again to provide her opera-like backing vocals, and Manzur gets another chance to shine with some nice flamenco-style guitar and trumpet in the break. According to Chiccarelli, speaking to *Radio.com* in 2014, the song more or less came about in the studio, where it was first considered B-side material, but eventually turned out to be one of the producer's favourite songs on the album. The lyrics are a plea to someone to leave his bride at the altar, as the singer suspects that she will treat him as a slave, urging him to 'write down every word I say'. This can be seen as another stab at the holy matrimony from Morrissey, along with songs like 'Will Never Marry'.

'Mountjoy' (Morrissey/Boorer)

This song takes its title from the Mountjoy Prison in Dublin. The moody musical backdrop, which is one long verse, suits the lyrics very well, as Morrissey tells the story of someone who spent some time in the prison. He name drops both 'The Joy', which is a nickname for Mountjoy, and Brendan Behan, a playwright and an IRA member who served some years here in the 1940s for an attempted murder of two detectives. Of course, Morrissey takes the opportunity to badmouth the legal system for the umpteenth time in the line, 'I was sent here by a three foot half-wit in a wig'.

'Oboe Concerto' (Morrissey/Boorer)

Despite its title, this song doesn't actually feature an oboe, but rather a clarinet, played by Boorer, who even gets to shine with a solo. The closing song of the original album is Morrissey's contemplation on his own mortality and that he is inevitably growing older – which is a common theme on his previous albums – but actually the first one on this record to see him address this subject. The song opens with a sample of comedian Rex Jameson and his character Mrs Shufflewick, which was very popular in the UK in the 50s and 60s. According to Chiccarelli on *Radio.com* in 2014, they had some videos of Jameson's performances in the studio, and they all enjoyed them a lot, so Morrissey decided to use a bit of it in the song.

'Scandinavia' (Morrissey/Boorer)

As usual these days, there was a deluxe edition of the album released on the same day as the regular one, with six bonus tracks. 'Scandinavia' is the first one of these, and this one had actually been available earlier as part of the extras on the *25Live* DVD, released in August 2013, as well as being played during a BBC radio session in 2011. This dramatic song, with choirs and pounding drums, has been interpreted by some fans as nationalistic, and that Morrissey is singing about how the Scandinavian countries have welcomed a lot of immigrants during the last decade or so; but that does seem far-fetched, despite his well-known political views. A more literal reading of the lyrics just sees a man who has no good feelings about the Scandinavian countries at all, but then suddenly changes his mind as he meets someone from there that he falls in love with. The last line can be interpreted as a homage to the Swedish national anthem, which contains the line: 'I want to live and I want to die in the North' ('Jag vill leva, jag vill dö i Norden').

'One of Our Own' (Morrissey/Manzur)

The second bonus track was written by Manzur, which comes as no surprise, as the swirling piano riff is prominent throughout the song. This is another one of Morrissey's flirts with the world of gangsters, and in the lyrics, we find someone standing at the tombstone of one of the gang members; a person who literally took a bullet for him, and now he wants to finish the job himself as he asks for the gun.

'Drag the River' (Morrissey/Boorer)

This story of a woman thinking about taking her own life by drowning herself in the river can be seen as a continuation of the theme in 'Mama Lay Softly on the River Bed' from *Years of Refusal*, or maybe even a prequel, as the woman here is probably still just contemplating suicide. The music was written by Boorer, and the song starts out with the splashing of waves against the shore before Moz is joined by an acoustic guitar for the verse, which would have been quite adequate backing for this tune. But sadly, they felt the need to add some distorted guitars and power chords for the chorus. Considering the lyrics, this would have done a lot better as a fully acoustic song.

'Forgive Someone' (Morrissey/Tobias)

The only song by Tobias among the bonus tracks, asks the question of if you really can forgive someone. In his much talked about interview with US talk show host Larry King in 2015, Morrissey said that he (sadly, according to himself) is a forgiving person, but that he doesn't stay friends with someone who had hurt him, which sounds quite reasonable to me. You could also see this as another song about the Mike Joyce court case, but that is probably taking it a bit too far. In true Tobias style, we get our fair share of power chords in this song as well, but it's still a nice tune.

'Julie in the Weeds' (Morrissey/Boorer)

Listening to the intro, you might think for a split second that Morrissey had turned to electronica for the first time, with the weird, fluttering electronic noises. But that soon changes, and the song instead evolves into a great pop tune, with a nice accordion touch. It would have been a perfect addition to the original album (actually, it would have been one of my highlights on it). The word 'weed' in the title has made some people suggest that Julie is smoking just that, making her forget all her troubles from youth; but that doesn't really sound like something Morrissey would write about, so it's most likely just about a girl that he wants to protect from her past and those who 'tell others what to do'.

'Art-hounds' (Morrissey/Boorer)

The final song on this bonus disc is a smoking, rocking pop song, with Morrissey sounding a bit like he did on *Southpaw Grammar*, only with a really good tune and better production. The song was only played once in concert, in London in August 2011, when Morrissey told the audience how to spell the title ('And for the six people who care, that song was called Art hyphen hounds, small 'h', Art-hounds'). In the lyrics, Morrissey pokes a finger at art critics who write and talk about things that they really know nothing about, and it's not hard to imagine that this is also a stab at music critics. The line 'If you cannot stand this fake world, take my hand', can also be seen as a reference to his own fans, as he's often seen as an escape from reality for them.

Low in High School (2017)

Personnel:
Morrissey: vocals
Boz Boorer: guitars
Jesse Tobias: guitars
Mando Lopez: bass guitar
Matt Walker: drums
Gustavo Manzur: keyboards, backing vocals
Roger Manning Jr: string and horn arrangements
Tony Molina: photography (front photo)
Jim Dyson: photography (Morrissey photo)
Max Joaquin Lopez: cover star
Recorded at La Fabrique (France), Forum Studios (Italy)
Produced by Joe Chiccarelli
Engineered by Davide Dell'Amore, Morgane Mayollet, Damien Arlot and Samuel Wahl
Playing time: 53:25
Label: BMG/Etienne (UK and US)
Release date: November 17 2017
Highest chart position: UK: 5, US: 20

The year following the release of *World Peace Is None of Your Business* was a turbulent year for Morrissey. In October 2014, he revealed that he had been diagnosed with Barrett's cancer, which attacks the oesophagus (or food pipe). Speaking to Larry King a year later, he said that the treatment had been effective and that he was still on medication, but that his health was 'blooming'.

In July 2015, he filed a sexual harassment suit against a security officer at the San Francisco International Airport, as Morrissey claimed that the officer had groped his genitalia during a security check before boarding a plane to London. The case was later dropped, as there was no evidence to prove that Morrissey was telling the truth.

A couple of months later, he finally published his first work of fiction, *List of the Lost,* and for most writers, that would probably be a joyous occasion. For Morrissey, it would turn out that hardly any critic liked the book, and it was met with mostly negative reviews – even though it was a bestseller in the UK for a period. In December 2015, the novel was given the unflattering 'Bad Sex Award' by the *Literary Review* magazine, especially for a sex scene that was discussed in length on social media during the autumn of 2015.

Then finally, more than three years after his latest album, Morrissey released his eleventh studio album, *Low in High School*, this time on yet another label, the major BMG, released in collaboration with Morrissey's own label, Etienne Records. When the press release regarding the album was sent out in August 2017, the spokesperson for BMG said that Morrissey was a 'dream signing for BMG', a statement they probably regretted a few years later. But more on that later on.

The album was once again recorded at La Fabrique in France, but also at the Forum in Italy, where *Ringleader of the Tormentors* was recorded a decade earlier. Joe Chiccarelli returned as producer, and the band was more or less the same, except that Mando Lopez (who played with indie rockers The Breeders when they reunited in the 2000s) replaced Solomon Walker on bass. Also, a former keyboard player with the band, Roger Manning Jr, returned to the team, this time as an arranger.

The album cover art proved to be controversial, as it depicts a boy holding an axe and a sign that says 'Axe the monarchy' (which could be seen as a wink to *The Queen Is Dead*). On the day of the album's release, the media reported that many record stores like HMV refused to stock the album due to the cover, but this was later denied by them.

As usual, the album was met with mixed reviews upon release, with some critics thinking it was his best album since *You Are the Quarry*, thirteen years earlier, while others thought that only really diehard Morrissey fans could enjoy the record. It did sell quite well, though, and yet again, Morrissey debuted in the UK top 10 (at #5). It also cracked the top 10 in Scotland, Ireland, and New Zealand, stalling at #20 in the US.

A year after the original release in December 2018, a deluxe edition came out, containing four new studio recordings and five live tracks, plus new artwork.

'My Love, I'd Do Anything for You' (Morrissey/Lopez)

New boy Lopez introduces himself straight away by writing the album opener, a heavy and frankly quite bland slow rocker, where Morrissey both attacks the mainstream media and dwells on his own loneliness. The opening line is rather relevant in these times of fake news, though: 'Teach your kids to recognize and despise all the propaganda.' I touched on the music in the beginning, and this is far from the best opener on a Moz album. The sound is fleshed out by trumpets and horns, but that doesn't really help a lot. This was released as the third single taken from the album on March 23, 2018.

'I Wish You Lonely' (Morrissey/Boorer)

This song was introduced live in the year before the release of the album, and it was also previewed as a digital stream in October 2017 as a teaser for the forthcoming full-length record. Here, Morrissey addresses loneliness, one of his all-time favourite subjects, as he wishes someone to be lonely just for a day, so that they can experience what he goes through day in and day out since the day he was born. He also sings about selfishness (as long as you get what you want and need, 'to hell with everybody else'), and in the final verse, he sings about the last humpback whale, that never gives up, despite being chased by Norwegian gunships – perhaps a metaphor for managing those hard times of loneliness.

'Jacky's Only Happy When She's Up on the Stage' (Morrissey/Boorer)

Released as the second single from the album on November 17, 2017, this one managed to get to the top of the UK Vinyl Singles Chart, and stayed there for two weeks at the end of that year. The lyrics tell the rather sad story about Jacky, an actress who evidently loves what she's doing, but she might not be that good at acting, considering that the audience all head for the exit when she's on stage. Some listeners thought that Morrissey was singing 'Brexit' instead of 'exit', but in an interview with *The Sunday Times* he denied this – even though later, in an interview his nephew Sam Esty Rayner (who did the music video for 'Kiss Me a Lot' a few years earlier) did with him for his official website in 2019, he claimed that he couldn't see anything attractive about the EU. In the music video, directed by Robert Hales (who previously won an MTV Music Award for his video for Gnarls Barkley's superhit 'Crazy' in 2006), the band is performing a very simple dance routine behind the singing Moz, with Boorer looking quite uncomfortable. There's been some speculation on whether Jacky is indeed Morrissey's older sister, Jacqueline, but he has neither denied nor confirmed this.

'Home Is a Question Mark' (Morrissey/Lopez)

This is another Lopez song, and this one is better than the first. It's based on an earlier song, written for *You Are the Quarry* by Alain Whyte, so there are actually three songwriters involved here. Musically, it's the slowest one on the album so far, with pounding drums and chiming guitars, plus a great intro with a twanging guitar and some jingle bells, for some reason. For someone who has had his fair share of moves during the past decades, it's not hard to understand that he finds it hard to pinpoint where his home is (but the line 'wrap your legs around my face just to greet me' is a bit open to interpretation, I must admit). That final note of the song, when he sings 'myself', is absolutely amazing!

'Spent the Day in Bed' (Morrissey/Manzur)

On September 18, 2017, Morrissey wrote his first-ever tweet, which just read 'Spent the day in bed...', and the next day it turned out to be the title of the first single from his forthcoming album. It would also be released as a 7' single, backed with a live cover of Ramones' classic, 'Judy Is a Punk'. And the song is quite far from your typical Morrissey tune – filled with electric piano, with an almost boogie-like groove from songwriter Manzur, and other electric sounds and strings – this one took many fans by surprise. But at the same time, it was probably just what he needed at this point in his career, to record something that sounded a bit fresh. The lyrics, hardly surprising considering the title, see Morrissey advocating to stay in bed to avoid the horrors of the modern world (including the media, of course), finishing with the mantra-like: 'No bus, no boss, no rain, no train.' It does sound nice, doesn't it? The music video, directed by Sophie Muller (who has won several awards for her videos, including No Doubt's 'Don't Speak' and Annie Lennox's 'Why'), shows Moz being pushed around in a wheelchair by footballer Joey Barton and then performing with his band while sitting on a chair (the song ends with him falling off it). The video was shot at the Peckham Liberal Club in South East London.

'I Bury the Living' (Morrissey/Tobias)

This album is in many ways very uncharacteristic Morrisseyone, as he's incorporating a lot of new sounds into his songs; and even if this isn't the most experimental song here, the electronic sounds that open the track (after the long intro), and then stay in the background almost all the way, are something that you probably wouldn't hear on a Moz album a decade earlier. The song, which is Tobias' first contribution to the album, is also a powerful anti-war statement, and the majestic choir segments only add to the power, with Morrissey singing about a soldier who can't be blamed for anything, as he's only following orders. The song ends with the tragic line: 'It's funny how the war goes on without our John.'

'In Your Lap' (Morrissey/Manzur)

From an anti-war track, we go straight to a song that celebrates the Arab Spring, and a beautiful one it is. Lines like: 'The people sing when the warlords all burn / Do not feel sad, it's simply their turn,' are really moving, considering the uprisings that are the subject of the song. The music was written by Manzur, and it really is his time to shine here, with some amazing piano playing – he had played bits of this song as interludes during concerts. The arrangement, with just the piano and howling wind, suits the lyrics very well too.

'The Girl From Tel Aviv Who Wouldn't Kneel' (Morrissey/Manzur)

The lyrics here are partly a tribute to Etty Hillesum (a Dutch Jewish writer, who died, aged 29, at the Auschwitz camp in 1943) and partly a tribute to Israel. In an interview with German newspaper, *Der Spiegel*, Morrissey said that he loved Tel-Aviv (he was actually given the keys to the city from the mayor in 2012) and that he felt that the boycotts towards Israel were wrong, as 'you should never judge a people by their government'. Musically, it's a piano-driven tango tune, with some Yiddish and Middle Eastern touches thrown in every now and then. It's another really experimental track.

'All the Young People Must Fall in Love' (Morrissey/Boorer)

Another uncharacteristic song, as it mainly consists of Morrissey's voice, handclaps, and an acoustic guitar, which gives it an almost folk-like touch. Boorer's tune is quite simple, and the song doesn't really have a distinct chorus; the lyrics are not the most obvious either. The easy way out when interpreting this song is to conclude that Morrissey thinks that the youth of today should try to forget all the uninteresting things happening around them and focus on love instead. Does that make any sense? Well, I'm not really sure. All in all, this isn't an album highlight. Still, it was released as the fourth and final single off the album on July 6, 2018.

'When You Open Your Legs' (Morrissey/Tobias)

For the second, but not last time on this album, Morrissey sings about Israel, and this time we're once again back in Tel-Aviv (a city often considered the 'gay capital of the Middle East'), where he gets thrown out of a club early in the morning. Introducing the song at a concert in 2017, he said that it's about 'human sexual love', which may come as no surprise, considering the title. The first thing that came to mind when I first saw the song title in the tracklist was that horrible sex scene in *List of the Lost*, and I guess I wasn't alone in having that feeling. The music shifts from having apparent Middle Eastern influences, to being a 'regular' pop song in the chorus, and it's quite clear that the guitarist has now left his earlier, power chord heavy style in favour of a more soft and relaxed songwriting approach.

'Who Will Protect Us From the Police?' (Morrissey/Boorer)

A few months before the album was released, Morrissey started selling a new t-shirt on his website, which had a pixelated photo of a police officer holding a person to the ground, presumably about to hit him. The t-shirt also bore the text: 'Who will protect us from the police?', which then turned out to be a song on his forthcoming album – a song that unsurprisingly dealt with police brutality. After the siren that kicks off the song, it evolves into yet another modern sounding tune, with heavy synth sounds in the verse, and a more traditional setup for the chorus. Boorer's melody isn't the most interesting, but it leaves Morrissey a bit more room to get his message through with a more powerful production, especially in the verses.

'Israel' (Morrissey/Manzur)

We're back in Israel again for this last song on the original album – there are nine more songs on the deluxe edition – and if you have listened to all the songs on the record, it comes as no surprise that Morrissey is a big fan of this country. This is a love song dedicated to Israel. The piano-based ballad is the second-longest on the album (only 'I Bury the Living' is longer, with its almost seven and a half minutes), and it's a suitably dramatic closing song, with pounding drums towards the end and Morrissey singing about how the rest of the world is jealous of Israel, but still insists on looking down on them.

'Lover-To-Be' (Morrissey/Boorer)

The first track of the bonus disc on the deluxe edition is this weird, groovy, Farfisa-filled song, which feels like a homage to The Doors more than anything else. Oddly enough, it wasn't written by organist Manzur, but by Boorer, and it's no wonder that this didn't make it to the original album. In the lyrics, Morrissey is posing himself as someone's lover-to-be, while ending the song with the line: 'I have trashed all the boozers in town, and now it's your turn,' which makes the whole story a bit contradictory. The song was eventually released as a limited edition 7' single for the worldwide Record Store Day event in 2019.

'Back on the Chain Gang' (Chrissie Hynde)

Originally recorded by The Pretenders and released as a single in September 1982, the song was written by their singer Chrissie Hynde, who is (was?) also a friend of Morrissey. The video for Morrissey's version (where he is seen playing a guitar, oddly enough) was available online on November 1, 2018, and later that same month, a 7' single was released. This could also be seen as a prequel to his next album, *California Sun*, which was an album of cover versions, though it did not feature 'Back on the Chain Gang'. Moz's take on the song doesn't differ a lot from the Pretenders version, so the experimental phase from *Low in High School* was perhaps put to rest here.

'Never Again Will I Be a Twin' (Morrissey/Lopez)

With its prominent, metallic sounding bassline, it comes as no surprise that this song was written by bassist Lopez. The lyrics, which in multiple metaphors tell the story of finally being free from your Siamese twin, can be interpreted to be about Johnny Marr and their relationship in the 80s, but also in a wider sense, to be about relationships and marriages in general. As for the former, this would hardly be the first song about Marr, and it's no secret that their once fabulous friendship ended abruptly when Marr left The Smiths. So, maybe what Moz is saying here is that he doesn't want to end up with another metaphorical twin, that he's good on his own, as we have heard before.

'This Song Doesn't End When It's Over' (Morrissey/Boorer)

In what could be a reference to the children's song, 'The Song That Doesn't End', this track finds Morrissey singing about a relationship that has fallen apart, but the singer still haunts his former lover's mind, even though he ends the song by exclaiming 'it's great to be out of your mind'. Musically, this Boorer tune is quite a dramatic ballad, with layers of fuzzy guitars and pounding drums. Yet again, it doesn't surprise me that this was left off the album.

'You'll Be Gone' (Elvis Presley/Red West/Charlie Hodge)

Originally recorded and co-written by Elvis Presley. His version was featured on the soundtrack to the *Girl Happy* movie in 1965, as well as being released as a single at the same time. Morrissey's cover was recorded live at his concert at the Eventim Apollo in London on September 20, 2015, and retains the flamenco feeling of the original recording – this version is more or less exactly the same as Elvis', with Moz's voice not being very far off from Mr Presley's as well. And we know from his Smiths days that he's a fan, considering the live rendition of 'His Latest Flame' (which was played as a medley with 'Rusholme Ruffians').

'Rose Garden' (live) (Joe South)
This country standard was originally written by Joe South, but was first recorded by Billy Joe Royal on his debut album in 1967 (an album that also contained the original version of 'Hush', later a hit for Deep Purple, and written by Royal). A few years later, country singer Lynn Anderson got a worldwide smash hit with her version. This is the version that Morrissey modelled his cover on, with an intro that isn't featured in either Royal's or South's 1968 recording of his own song. The live version featured here was appropriately enough recorded when Morrissey played the iconic country stage at the Grand Ole Opry in Nashville on July 2, 2015.

'Are You Sure Hank Done It This Way?' (live) (Waylon Jennings)
Morrissey stays in the land of country music on this two-chord Waylon Jennings cover. Jennings released the song as a single in 1975, giving him his fourth number one single on the country chart as a solo artist. The Hank in the song refers to Hank Williams Sr, with the lyrics suggesting that country music got a bit too busy with rhinestones and glamour in the 70s, thus the song's title. The live version on this bonus disc was recorded in Visalia, California, on August 29, 2015, and is a bit heavier than Jennings' version, with electric guitars, but it's still very much the same song.

'I Didn't Know What To Do' (live) (Gilbert O'Sullivan)
I think many Morrissey fans said the very same thing when they told their friends that their idol had played a Gilbert O'Sullivan song when they went to his concert. Irish singer-songwriter O'Sullivan isn't the coolest artist to cover; let's agree on that. But for me, I think it's a great choice, and Gilbert should have far more credibility than he has. O'Sullivan's version was released on the B-side to his single 'We Will' in 1971, and once again, Morrissey's version is quite true to the original; just like 'Rose Garden', he decided to cover it at a very suitable place, at the 3Arena in Dublin (on December 1, 2014), a few hours from O'Sullivan's hometown of Waterford. He also covered 'Nothing Rhymed' and 'Alone Again (Naturally)' during other Dublin shows, so I think it's fair to say that Moz is a Gilbert fan.

'Judy Is a Punk' (live) (Joey Ramone)
So, after covering two country songs, an Elvis track and a Gilbert O'Sullivan B-side, Morrissey turned to the 70s punk scene and covered this classic Ramones song, originally released on their debut album in 1976. Morrissey and the band played this song quite a lot during shows in 2016-2018, and this

recording was made at the Orchard Hall in Tokyo on September 29, 2016, where it was played as the encore. As the band is usually keen to rock out, this song suits them quite well, but there's something about Morrissey's voice here that makes me feel that it's a bit misplaced. It's also a rather bad idea for middle-aged men to play this kind of energetic punk. Despite all this, it was released as the B-side on the 'Spent The Day in Bed' single.

California Son (2019)

Personnel:
Morrissey: vocals
Boz Boorer: guitars, mandolin
Jesse Tobias: various guitars
David Levita: acoustic guitar (on 'Don't Interrupt the Sorrow')
Zac Rae: organ, upright piano, keyboards (on 'Days of Decision', 'Lenny's Tune', 'Suffer the Little Children' and 'Some Say I Got Devil')
Mando Lopez: bass guitar (except on 'It's Over' and 'Loneliness Remembers What Happiness Forgets')
Sean Hurley: bass guitar on 'It's Over' and 'Loneliness Remembers What Happiness Forgets'
Matt Walker: drums, drum programming
Gustavo Manzur: synthesizers, accordion
Roger Manning Jr: string and horn arrangements, keyboards, synthesizers, backing vocals
Steve Aho: orchestration
Liam Lynch: sleeve design,
Michael Muller: photography
Recorded at Sunset Sound, Hollywood (US)
Produced by Joe Chiccarelli
Engineered by Chris Dugan, Tim Kvasnosky, Marcus Paquin, and Samuel Wahl
Playing time: 40:08
Label: BMG/Etienne (UK and US)
Release date: May 24 2019
Highest chart position: UK: 4, US: 95

During the tour that followed the release of *Low in High School,* Morrissey began playing quite a few more or less unexpected covers as part of the set (he had done this earlier too, but now it seemed to be a bit more of a regular part of the shows), and the bonus disc that came with the deluxe edition of that album also showed his newfound love of playing songs by his idols. But despite this, I don't think his fans would ever expect him to record an album worth of covers. But he did.

Ever since the mid-2010s, Morrissey had been more and more outspoken about his political views, which tended to lean to the right, seemingly going further out on that wing every year. These views also resulted in boycotts from both shops, media and fans, who thought that his support of the far-right party, *For Britain* (he wore their badge when he played on Jimmy Fallon's popular talk show in the US in May 2019), was a bit too much for them. So maybe that was one of the reasons Morrissey chose to make his next album a record full of other people's songs, as he might have thought it was a bad time for writing personal lyrics.

The album was recorded at the Sunset Studios in Hollywood, California, during the summer of 2018, and the backing band was the same as on *Low in*

High School. He also enlisted Joe Chiccarelli as the producer for the third time in a row, also bringing in a lot of special guests, both backing vocalists and musicians, including Green Day singer Billie Joe Armstrong.

The first news regarding the album came out in September 2018, when some photos of Morrissey and American singer-songwriter Lauro Pergolizzi (known by her initials, LP) posing with basketballs were published on Moz's official website, with a mention of a new album in the making. But it wasn't until late 2018 that the album title and tracklist was published, and a few months later, in February 2019, the first single, the Roy Orbison cover 'It's Over', was sent out to radio stations and media. Just one physical single was released from the album when 'Wedding Bell Blues' (written by Laura Nyro) came out on 7' in May 2019.

A few weeks before the album release, Morrissey played at the Lunt-Fontanne Theatre on Broadway for seven nights (from May 2 to 11), where he previewed some of the songs from the album, as well as providing the audience with a retrospective of his entire career, both solo and with The Smiths. After the release of the album, Moz embarked on a tour of North America during the autumn of 2019.

The reviews of the album were mostly mixed or negative, with quite a few reviewers saying that it was hard to separate Morrissey the person from Morrissey the artist, considering his political views. But even though they found it difficult to enjoy his albums as much as they used to, they couldn't deny that his voice was still as powerful as ever.

'Morning Starship' (Bruce Wayne Campbell)

The opening song on the album was originally written and recorded by Jobriath (Bruce Wayne Campbell), who was the first openly gay artist to sign to a major record label, and when he died of AIDS in 1983, he was one of the first internationally known musicians to do so. 'Morning Starship' was included on his first solo album in 1973 (he released an album with the band Pidgeon in 1969 as well), which made him part of the then very popular glam rock scene, not far from what David Bowie was doing at the time. Actually, Morrissey was the curator for the first-ever Jobriath CD compilation, *Lonely Planet Boy* (2004), so he was obviously a fan already. On Morrissey's version of the song, the rock has been given softer edges, with a harpsichord playing in the background, while the guitars are doing their best to howl and enrich the track.

'Don't Interrupt the Sorrow' (Joni Mitchell)

So from Jobriath, we go to the quintessential female singer-songwriter, Joni Mitchell, and a song that was originally included on her album, *The Hissing of Summer Lawns*, which came out in 1975. Before the release of *California Son*, Morrissey claimed that it was an album of protest songs, which might be stretching it a bit, but Mitchell's lyrics here can absolutely be seen as feminist, as she sings about women liberating themselves from male dominance.

Morrissey's recording of the song is done in the same style as Joni's, but the sound has been fleshed out with electric piano (making it a bit groovier than the original recording), discreet synthesizer noises, and a saxophone solo, played by Tom Scott. Ariel Engle from indie rockers Broken Social Scene also joins in on backing vocals.

'Only a Pawn in a Game' (Bob Dylan)

This Bob Dylan cover (it was originally released on his *The Times They Are A-Changin* album in 1964) is probably the most problematic song on the album, especially in the light of Morrissey's statements during the past years. The lyrics tell the story of how civil-rights activist Medgar Evers was killed by Byron De La Beckwith in June 1963 in what could only be described as a racist killing, but Dylan somehow manages to make De La Beckwith a victim too, as he was 'only a pawn in the game'. Maybe Dylan himself also found his lyrics a bit inappropriate after a while since he stopped playing it later in 1964. His original recording contains just him and his acoustic guitar, but Moz and his band instead base it on organ, accordion and pounding drums. Once again, he gets some help with the backing vocals, this time from another indie rocker, Ed Droste, from the band Grizzly Bear.

'Suffer the Little Children' (Buffy Sainte-Marie)

It's hard not to comment on the fact that The Smiths recorded the similarly titled original song 'Suffer Little Children' for their debut album in 1984, and I suppose that Morrissey was well aware of that when he chose to cover this Buffy Sainte-Marie song. She recorded the song for her 1969 album *Illuminations,* an album that found her moving away from her folk roots and instead experimenting with electronic sounds. But on this particular song, it's just Buffy and her guitar, playing a melody that's a bit hard to grasp due to a lot of unexpected chord changes. Morrissey's version sounds more like a show tune, with a thundering piano (played by Zac Rae) in the background, handclaps, and tuba (played by Devon Taylor), but it suits the song quite well!

'Days of Decision' (Phil Ochs)

If Morrissey wanted to make an album full of protest songs, he did the right thing to include the best protest singer of them all, Phil Ochs, who recorded this song for his second album, *I Ain't Marching Any More* (1965). But, on the other hand, Ochs was famous for being an outspoken activist for human rights and anti-racism. Ochs' version is just like many other protest songs from the 60s, formulated with just his voice and his guitar, while Morrissey once again decides to flesh out the sound on his rendition with drums, slide guitars and keyboards, along with Manzur's and Boorer's acoustic guitars. The backing vocals are provided by Sameer Gadhia from the band Young the Giant.

'It's Over' (Roy Orbison/Bill Dees)
If we return to Morrissey's statement that this is a protest song album, this one is a bit hard to fit into that category. The song was written by Roy Orbison, released as a single in April 1964 (peaking at #1 in the UK a few months later), and contains one of the few lyrics on this album that Morrissey could have written himself, as it deals with heartache and loneliness, two very familiar subjects for Moz. This cover version sounds quite a lot like Orbison's original, and it really shows off Morrissey's amazing voice, even hitting the high notes in the chorus. LP joins him on backing vocals for this song, and Sean Hurley sits in on bass.

'Wedding Bell Blues' (Laura Nyro)
Written by an eighteen-year-old Laura Nyro in 1966 (and recorded for her debut album *More Than a Discovery* that same year), it wasn't until The 5th Dimension recorded their version in 1969 that it became a hit (peaking at #1 in the US and #16 in the UK). Both those versions are quite similar when it came to the arrangement, and Morrissey's rendition follows the beaten path, with the album's special guest star, Green Day's Billie Joe Armstrong, lending his voice for some vocal harmonies (there's actually a bunch of people singing backup, including Lydia Night from punk band the Regrettes). I think that Roger Manning Jr's tinkering piano deserves to be mentioned here as well. It was released as the first and only single from the album on April 8 2019, and a month later, it was also available as a coloured 7' single.

'Loneliness Remembers What Happiness Forgets' (Burt Bacharach/Hal David)
Judging from the title, this could be an original Morrissey composition, but it was written by Burt Bacharach and Hal David, and first recorded by New Zealand singer Allison Durbin in 1969 for her album *Soft & Soulful*, then later by Dionne Warwick for her album *I'll Never Fall in Love Again* in 1971. The credits on 'California Son' actually says that Warwick recorded it first, which is incorrect. Morrissey's cover more or less copies the arrangement from the previous two versions, complete with synth strings and horns, and this seems to be a song much more up his alley than political protest songs, as he talks quite a lot about his love for this kind of easy listening in his autobiography.

'Lady Willpower' (Jerry Fuller)
Written by songwriter and producer Jerry Fuller, and originally recorded by Gary Puckett & the Union Gap (probably best known for the hit single 'Young Girl') for the album *Incredible* in 1968, this is another song on this album where Morrissey decided to keep the original arrangement as good as untouched. The horns, arranged by Roger Manning Jr, are still there, and there's even a trumpet solo, played by Danny Levin, along with the stomping

rhythm. The lyrics sound a bit questionable these days, as they concern a man who's a bit annoyed that the woman he loves doesn't seem to want to have sex with him. Poor Moz.

'When You Close Your Eyes' (Carly Simon/Billy Mernit)
It's nice to see that Morrissey picked so many songs by female singer-songwriters for this album, and here's another one, co-written and recorded by Carly Simon for her hit album *No Secrets* (which also spawned the hit single 'You're So Vain') in 1972. In this case, Morrissey takes a step away from the original arrangement and uses programmed drums and synthesizers as the main instruments. For this song, he is joined by Petra Haden (former member of That Dog, and The Decemberists) on backing vocals, and also the dog Little Willie, who 'sings' during the intro.

'Lenny's Tune' (Tim Hardin)
American singer-songwriter Tim Hardin was famous for being very inconsistent, mostly because of his heavy use of drugs, and it's more evident than ever on his fourth album, *Tim Hardin 3 Live in Concert*, which was recorded live at The Town Hall in New York in April 1968. The album also contains the only official release of this song, written about the death of comedian Lenny Bruce, who died in August 1966. Morrissey's version is, because of its stripped-down arrangement (just a piano, bass and a mandolin), a lot more enjoyable than Hardin's original recording, and he also shortened the song to three and half minutes, where the original is almost seven minutes long.

'Some Say I Got Devil' (Melanie Safka)
The last song of this album was written and recorded by Melanie Safka, mostly known by just her first name, for her breakthrough album *Gather Me* in 1971 (which also contained her hit single 'Brand New Key'). The lyrics to the song have been interpreted in different ways through the years, as she first claims to indeed have the devil in her, but then in the next line says 'some say I got angel'. So, I guess it's up to the listeners to make what they want of it. Morrissey's cover replaces the original's fingerpicking guitar with piano, bombastic drums, and trumpets (played by both Manzur and Danny Levin), making it a powerful album closer.

Related Track
'Brow of My Beloved' (Morrissey/Boorer)
Wait a minute… a Morrissey original on a covers album? Well, this song was released on the B-side on the 'Wedding Bell Blues' single and then came out as a digital-only single in July 2019, so it seems fitting to include it as a 'bonus track' on this album (it was also recorded during the 'California Son' sessions at Sunset Studio). The song kicks off with an atmospheric bleeping synthesizer,

probably courtesy of Gustavo Manzur, who keeps adding flourishes of bleeps throughout the song that make it stand out a bit from other Morrissey tracks. Lyrically, we're back to all too familiar hunting grounds, with self-pity and a longing for love.

I Am Not a Dog on a Chain (2020)

Personnel:
Morrissey: vocals
Boz Boorer: guitars, mandolin, saxophone, zither, clarinet, string arrangements
Jesse Tobias: various guitars, electric sitar
Mando Lopez: bass guitar (except on 'What Kind of People Live in These Houses?')
Sean Hurley: bass guitar on 'What Kind of People Live in These Houses?'
Matt Walker: percussion
Gustavo Manzur: synthesizers, accordion, guitar, mellotron, drum programming, piano, backing vocals
Roger Manning Jr: harmonium, horn, mellotron, organ, piano, string arrangements, synthesizers, backing vocals
Joe Chiccarelli: drum programming, synthesizer
Liam Lynch: sleeve design
Chris Stewart: photography (cover)
John Fekner: photography
Recorded at Studio La Fabrique, Saint-Rémy-de-Provence (France)
Produced by Joe Chiccarelli
Engineered by Joe Chiccarelli and Miro La Gagioia
Playing time: 49:26
Label: BMG/Etienne (UK and US)
Release date: March 20 2020
Highest chart position: UK: 3, US Independent Chart: 44

Since 'California Son' was released almost a year after the recording sessions took place in Hollywood, Morrissey and his band had all of 2019 to prepare for the next album while playing live on the North America tour, undertaken during the autumn that same year. Oddly enough, he didn't take the opportunity to preview some of the new songs during this tour, but he did manage to perform a few live dates in Germany and the UK in March 2020 before the coronavirus pandemic really hit in Europe that same month, and all live music was cancelled for the rest of the year. Later in 2020, Morrissey's mother, Elisabeth, passed away. This was a really tough blow for Morrissey – when she was ill, he even asked his fans to go out and pray for her. As had been the case for the past albums, the band was intact, and Joe Chiccarelli stayed in the control room for his fourth consecutive album. Just like on *California Son*, there were many guests in the studio, providing everything from backing vocals and trumpets to fiddles and laughter.

The album was recorded at the La Fabrique studio in Provence, France, just like *World Peace Is None of Your Business*, and *Low in High School*, and since Morrissey's last album had been a record of other people's songs, he had spent the last years writing the lyrics for this new album. And he was definitely back in true Moz style, with songs dealing with subjects like suicide, animal rights, and the media.

The reviews for the album were mixed, to say the least, and some of the reviewers said that the lyrics were his weakest yet; that he insisted on being a 'victim' in this modern world. That being said, *NME* said that it was his best album in years (but they still had a hard time in separating the artist from the person), with many critics saying that his voice was still his greatest asset.

This album would prove to be his last for BMG, as it was reported in November 2020 that Morrissey's deal with them had expired, and they didn't intend on renewing it. So that means that at the time of writing this, Moz is once again without a record deal, and many fans thought that this might have been his very last album. But then in late May 2021, Morrissey announced on his official website that he had recorded a new album, entitled *Bonfire of Teenagers*, but he was still without a label, offering the album to the highest (or lowest) bidding label.

On August 28, 2021, he began a short residency at The Colosseum At Caesar's Palace in Las Vegas, where he treated the audience to some lesser-played songs, like 'Tomorrow' and 'Ouija Board, Ouija Board', and also rarely played Smiths songs like 'This Night Has Opened My Eyes' and 'Never Had No One Ever'.

'Jim Jim Falls' (Morrissey/Tobias)

The Jim Jim Falls are located in the North of Australia and plunge up to 200 metres down to the creek below. In this song, Morrissey pictures someone who's standing at the edge, considering jumping to their untimely death – in a way echoing the lyrics to 'Shakespeare's Sister' and 'Angel, Angel, Down We Go Together', while he's doing his best to make them do it ('If you're gonna kill yourself, then for God's sake, just kill yourself'). Musically, the most ear-catching part of the song is probably Manning Jr's synth backing, which opens the song and then stays in the background the whole time, with a surge that makes it sound a bit like 'Life Is a Pigsty'.

'Love Is on Its Way Out' (Morrissey/Manzur)

I don't think any Morrissey fan could imagine ten or fifteen years ago that this is what he would sound like in the future. Back then, Moz was known for being a conservative guy (in music as well as politics), but somewhere along the line, something happened. Either he broadened his musical taste, or someone said that this was the right thing to do if you wanted to appeal to younger listeners. In this song, which finds him mourning the state of the world (with nerve gassed children and rich people shooting elephants and lions), the synthesizer once again takes centre stage, at least to start with. Later on, drums, guitars, and mellotron join in as well, resulting in a somewhat chaotic ending. The song was also released as the second digital-only single from the album on January 31, 2020.

'Bobby, Don't You Think They Know?' (Morrissey/Manzur)

Before the release of the album, this was the most talked-about song on it, as it features singer Thelma Houston (probably best known for the iconic disco hit 'Don't Leave Me This Way' in 1977) on backing vocals. It was also released as the first single on January 10 2020, and surely took many fans by surprise when they first heard it. During almost six minutes, it hops from being yet another electronica song, with a very prominent synth bass line, to being piano-based, and then suddenly we get a saxophone solo (courtesy of Boorer), a squealing organ solo, and finally a guitar solo. Add to that the somewhat nonsensical lyrics about a person who's deep down in drug abuse, though he tries to hide it, and you get what might not be the typical first preview from a forthcoming album. But then again, Morrissey always goes his own way, for good and for bad.

'I Am Not a Dog on a Chain' (Morrissey/Tobias)

No other song on this album sums up Morrissey in 2020 like this one, at least when it comes to the lyrics. Here, he says that he has his own views and that we shouldn't read newspapers as they are all troublemakers. He also sings that we should seek the truth in what's not shown to us, and after half the song, I think he sounds more like an internet troll than the Morrissey I learned to love almost 30 years ago, which is sad. And musically... well, it sounds more like a demo recording than a finished song, as the verse (or is it the chorus?) sounds unfinished and seems to lack an element or two. It's not his strongest effort.

'What Kind of People Live in These Houses?' (Morrissey/Tobias)

Listening to this song for the first time, I instantly checked the songwriting credits to see if Alain Whyte had made a surprising comeback, but no, it was written by Tobias, even though its jangly and poppy tune sounds like something from Morrissey's prime solo years in the mid-90s. Too bad then that the lyrics are cynical Moz at his worst, as he walks around in the rough neighbourhoods in his city (probably Los Angeles), wondering how people can survive living the lives they live and voting the way they vote. Lucky for him that he could return home to his mansion after the walk...

'Knockabout World' (Morrissey/Tobias)

Electronic Morrissey is back, with an intro that makes me think of both 'It Takes a Muscle To Fall in Love' by Dutch duo Spectral Display and the classic 'Only You' by Yazoo (though the guitars come in for the chorus). Written by Tobias, it's nice to see that he can still write these kinds of songs too, and not just the more muscular rock tracks that he provided for his first albums with Moz. Lyrically, it's back to the outsiders and the misunderstood, as Moz congratulates someone on surviving, even though people tried to make him or her into a 'public target'. Maybe he's singing to himself? That wouldn't surprise me, considering that he often thinks of himself as a victim. This song was released as the third and final digital single from the album on February 21 2020.

'Darling, I Hug a Pillow' (Morrissey/Lopez)
This album certainly finds Morrissey leaping from one subject to another, and some of them are classic Moz, like this one about longing for love and closeness. The title makes me think of the lines Morrissey is singing during the outro of 'Some Girls Are Bigger Than Others', which were borrowed from the Johnny Tillotson song 'Send Me the Pillow You Dream On', but this time it's Moz who's using the pillow. Musically, the most notable feature is Danny Levin's trumpet and Sally Chae's backing vocals, and while the verse isn't too bad, the chorus is weirdly tuneless. I doubt that this is anyone's favourite song off the album.

'Once I Saw the River Clean' (Morrissey/Tobias)
This song is like the perfect combination of the new and old Morrissey – a partly electronic backing for lyrics about his childhood in Manchester, where he paints the picture of him walking with his grandma to Chester Road to buy the 'Metal Guru' single by T Rex, and then to Talbot Road to walk and play among the graves. Bridget Regan's fiddle in the middle of the song also adds a touch of days past and actually blends well with the more modern-sounding rhythms. Sure, this might seem like very typical Morrissey lyrics, but oh how I wish he could write more songs like this instead of acting like an offended man on Twitter. This might not be the best tune of the album, but lyric-wise it's surely among the best.

'The Truth About Ruth' (Morrissey/Manzur)
Undoubtedly, Morrissey has a lot of views that are controversial, to say the least, but despite this, he has always been a supporter of the LGBT community, often talking about inspirational people like Jobriath (whose song 'Morning Starship' he covered on the 'California Son' album). In this song, he really sings their praise, saying that the world is 'ill-prepared for the truth about Ruth' and that 'Ruth is John'. The piano-based melody tells us that this was written by Manzur (his third and final contribution to this album), but the sound is also fleshed out with the usual suspects and some mandolin and zither from Boorer. It's perhaps not a highlight of the album, but it's a decent song with important lyrics. That's good enough for me.

'The Secret of Music' (Morrissey/Lopez)
Remember when Morrissey surprised all his fans by including two marathon songs on *Southpaw Grammar*? Well, here we go again, with a song that's nearly eight minutes long, and this time it's a bit more experimental, both when it comes to the music and the lyrics. Musically, the song has been described as hypnotic and psychedelic, and I have to agree with that. The drums almost sound like an infinite loop (they were indeed programmed by Chiccarelli, who also helps out with the synths on this song), and while they are pounding away, guitars are distorted and scattered all over the place, on

top of which, Tobias and Daniel Cayotte are reciting texts, with two women (Rose Mary and Megan Sluiter) laughing in the background every now and then. Does this sound a bit trippy to you? Well, it is. And the lyrics don't help to make that experience any milder either. 'Bum, bum bum, the drum / Cymbals symbolize your mind / I think you should try / Classical guitar'. Enough said. I'm a bit surprised that he didn't put this song last on the album, though.

'My Hurling Days Are Gone' (Morrissey/Tobias)
So, here we are. The last song on what might turn out to be Morrissey's last album. Once again he looks back at his childhood (with images of his mum and a teddy bear), contemplating that fact that he's not getting any younger, and concluding that time will send you an invoice that you will pay with your eyesight, legs, strength and voice (well, he still has his voice, so maybe he will pay with strength and legs instead then). For the second time, Morrissey has brought a children's choir, the Glendale Tab & Apple Choir, into the studio for this song (he first did it on the *Ringleader of the Tormentors* album), and they give the song a very nostalgic and warm atmosphere. Will this be the last new Morrissey song ever released? I doubt it. But it might be the last song on the last officially released album. If so, he could definitely have ended it all in far worse a way.

Contemporary Singles

Honey, You Know Where To Find Me (10' single, 2020)

Personnel:
Morrissey: vocals
Boz Boorer: guitars
Alain Whyte: guitars
Jonny Bridgwood: bass guitar
Spencer James Cobrin: drums

This limited edition 10' single was released for the worldwide event Record Store Day on August 20th 2020, and it features three songs from the *Southpaw Grammar* sessions in 1995 (though 'Fantastic Bird' was actually recorded during the *Your Arsenal* sessions in 1992). All three songs were added to the parent album when it was reissued and expanded in 2009.

Cosmic Dancer with David Bowie (single, 2020)

Personnel:
Morrissey: vocals
David Bowie: vocals
Boz Boorer: guitar
Alain Whyte: guitar
Jonny Bridgwood: bass guitar
Spencer James Cobrin: drums

'Cosmic Dancer' (Marc Bolan)

An earlier live recording of this T Rex cover was released as a B-side to 'Pregnant for the Last Time' in 1991, a recording made just a month before this one, which was taped at the Great Western Forum in Los Angeles on 2nd June 1991. Bowie's appearance on stage to sing the song was a surprise to the audience, which is quite obvious when you listen to the recording. The single was released as digital-only on November 13, 2020, with a limited edition 7' single following on February 19, 2021.

'That's Entertainment' (Paul Weller)

On the sleeve, this is called '2021 version', which means that it's not just a re-release of the recording that was released as a B-side on 'Sing Your Life' in 1991. This cover of The Jam's old classic was frequently played live by Morrissey in the early 90s, but this is a studio recording (just like the earlier release). According to a press release going out in February 2021, this new version is based on a recording Morrissey and his band did of the song in 1994. That session was allegedly aborted, but they kept Moz's vocal track, and then Boz Boorer added some new instrumentation and backing vocals on this 2021 version.

Sources

Goddard, Simon: *Mozipedia – The Encyclopedia of Morrissey and The Smiths* (Ebury, 2012)
Marr, Johnny: *Set The Boy Free – The Autobiography* (Arrow Books, 2016)
Morrissey: *Autobiography* (Penguin, 2013)
Rogan, Johnny: *Morrissey and Marr – The Severed Alliance* (Omnibus Press, 1993)
Rogan, Johnny: *The Smiths – The Visual Documentary* (Omnibus Press, 1994)
Rogan, Johnny: *The Complete Guide to the Music of The Smiths & Morrissey* (Omnibus Press, 1995)
Rogan, Johnny: *Morrissey: The Albums* (Omnibus Press, 2006)
www.morrissey-solo.com
www.morrisseyofficial.com
www.songfacts.com
www.wikipedia.org

On Track series

Tori Amos – Lisa Torem 978-1-78952-142-9
Asia – Peter Braidis 978-1-78952-099-6
Barclay James Harvest – Keith and Monica Domone 978-1-78952-067-5
The Beatles – Andrew Wild 978-1-78952-009-5
The Beatles Solo 1969-1980 – Andrew Wild 978-1-78952-030-9
Blue Oyster Cult – Jacob Holm-Lupo 978-1-78952-007-1
Marc Bolan and T.Rex – Peter Gallagher 978-1-78952-124-5
Kate Bush – Bill Thomas 978-1-78952-097-2
Camel – Hamish Kuzminski 978-1-78952-040-8
Caravan – Andy Boot 978-1-78952-127-6
Cardiacs – Eric Benac 978-1-78952-131-3
Eric Clapton Solo – Andrew Wild 978-1-78952-141-2
The Clash – Nick Assirati 978-1-78952-077-4
Crosby, Stills and Nash – Andrew Wild 978-1-78952-039-2
The Damned – Morgan Brown 978-1-78952-136-8
Deep Purple and Rainbow 1968-79 – Steve Pilkington 978-1-78952-002-6
Dire Straits – Andrew Wild 978-1-78952-044-6
The Doors – Tony Thompson 978-1-78952-137-5
Dream Theater – Jordan Blum 978-1-78952-050-7
Elvis Costello and The Attractions – Georg Purvis 978-1-78952-129-0
Emerson Lake and Palmer – Mike Goode 978-1-78952-000-2
Fairport Convention – Kevan Furbank 978-1-78952-051-4
Peter Gabriel – Graeme Scarfe 978-1-78952-138-2
Genesis – Stuart MacFarlane 978-1-78952-005-7
Gentle Giant – Gary Steel 978-1-78952-058-3
Gong – Kevan Furbank 978-1-78952-082-8
Hawkwind – Duncan Harris 978-1-78952-052-1
Roy Harper – Opher Goodwin 978-1-78952-130-6
Iron Maiden – Steve Pilkington 978-1-78952-061-3
Jefferson Airplane – Richard Butterworth 978-1-78952-143-6
Jethro Tull – Jordan Blum 978-1-78952-016-3
Elton John in the 1970s – Peter Kearns 978-1-78952-034-7
The Incredible String Band – Tim Moon 978-1-78952-107-8
Iron Maiden – Steve Pilkington 978-1-78952-061-3
Judas Priest – John Tucker 978-1-78952-018-7
Kansas – Kevin Cummings 978-1-78952-057-6
Led Zeppelin – Steve Pilkington 978-1-78952-151-1
Level 42 – Matt Philips 978-1-78952-102-3
Aimee Mann – Jez Rowden 978-1-78952-036-1
Joni Mitchell – Peter Kearns 978-1-78952-081-1
The Moody Blues – Geoffrey Feakes 978-1-78952-042-2
Mike Oldfield – Ryan Yard 978-1-78952-060-6
Tom Petty – Richard James 978-1-78952-128-3
Porcupine Tree – Nick Holmes 978-1-78952-144-3
Queen – Andrew Wild 978-1-78952-003-3
Radiohead – William Allen 978-1-78952-149-8
Renaissance – David Detmer 978-1-78952-062-0
The Rolling Stones 1963-80 – Steve Pilkington 978-1-78952-017-0

Also available from Sonicbond ...

The Smiths and Morrissey – Tommy Gunnarsson 978-1-78952-140-5
Steely Dan – Jez Rowden 978-1-78952-043-9
Steve Hackett – Geoffrey Feakes 978-1-78952-098-9
Thin Lizzy – Graeme Stroud 978-1-78952-064-4
Toto – Jacob Holm-Lupo 978-1-78952-019-4
U2 – Eoghan Lyng 978-1-78952-078-1
UFO – Richard James 978-1-78952-073-6
The Who – Geoffrey Feakes 978-1-78952-076-7
Roy Wood and the Move – James R Turner 978-1-78952-008-8
Van Der Graaf Generator – Dan Coffey 978-1-78952-031-6
Yes – Stephen Lambe 978-1-78952-001-9
Frank Zappa 1966 to 1979 – Eric Benac 978-1-78952-033-0
10CC – Peter Kearns 978-1-78952-054-5

Decades Series
The Bee Gees in the 1960s – Andrew Mon Hughes et al 978-1-78952-148-1
Alice Cooper in the 1970s – Chris Sutton 978-1-78952-104-7
Curved Air in the 1970s – Laura Shenton 978-1-78952-069-9
Fleetwood Mac in the 1970s – Andrew Wild 978-1-78952-105-4
Focus in the 1970s – Stephen Lambe 978-1-78952-079-8
Genesis in the 1970s – Bill Thomas 978178952-146-7
Marillion in the 1980s – Nathaniel Webb 978-1-78952-065-1
Pink Floyd In The 1970s – Georg Purvis 978-1-78952-072-9
The Sweet in the 1970s – Darren Johnson 978-1-78952-139-9
Uriah Heep in the 1970s – Steve Pilkington 978-1-78952-103-0
Yes in the 1980s – Stephen Lambe with David Watkinson 978-1-78952-125-2

On Screen series
Carry On… – Stephen Lambe 978-1-78952-004-0
David Cronenberg – Patrick Chapman 978-1-78952-071-2
Doctor Who: The David Tennant Years – Jamie Hailstone 978-1-78952-066-8
Monty Python – Steve Pilkington 978-1-78952-047-7
Seinfeld Seasons 1 to 5 – Stephen Lambe 978-1-78952-012-5

Other Books
Babysitting A Band On The Rocks – G.D. Praetorius 978-1-78952-106-1
Derek Taylor: For Your Radioactive Children – Andrew Darlington 978-1-78952-038-5
Iggy and The Stooges On Stage 1967-1974 – Per Nilsen 978-1-78952-101-6
Jon Anderson and the Warriors – the road to Yes – David Watkinson 978-1-78952-059-0
Nu Metal: A Definitive Guide – Matt Karpe 978-1-78952-063-7
Tommy Bolin: In and Out of Deep Purple – Laura Shenton 978-1-78952-070-5
Maximum Darkness – Deke Leonard 978-1-78952-048-4
Maybe I Should've Stayed In Bed – Deke Leonard 978-1-78952-053-8
Psychedelic Rock in 1967 – Kevan Furbank 978-1-78952-155-9
The Twang Dynasty – Deke Leonard 978-1-78952-049-1

and many more to come!

Would you like to write for Sonicbond Publishing?

We are mainly a music publisher, but we also occasionally publish in other genres including film and television. At Sonicbond Publishing we are always on the look-out for authors, particularly for our two main series, On Track and Decades.

Mixing fact with in depth analysis, the On Track series examines the entire recorded work of a particular musical artist or group. All genres are considered from easy listening and jazz to 60s soul to 90s pop, via rock and metal.

The Decades series singles out a particular decade in an artist or group's history and focuses on that decade in more detail than may be allowed in the On Track series.

While professional writing experience would, of course, be an advantage, the most important qualification is to have real enthusiasm and knowledge of your subject. First-time authors are welcomed, but the ability to write well in English is essential.

Sonicbond Publishing has distribution throughout Europe and North America, and all our books are also published in E-book form. Authors will be paid a royalty based on sales of their book. Further details about our books are available from www.sonicbondpublishing.com. To contact us, complete the contact form there or email info@sonicbondpublishing.co.uk